"I remember my first major crisis a[...]
God had brought a sweet mento[...]
walked this path before me, and I[...]
with much pain. I cannot imagine how I would have navigated my own story without her example, showing me, it was possible. Carole Leathem's book, *Finding Joy in My Messy Life*, is one woman's walk of faith in a crisis she never anticipated or wanted as a part of her story: the mental illness of her husband. She had no one to talk to when this occurred and understands what it is to face this journey alone. Now, she has transparently and honestly told her story, offering encouragement and practical tips to help you in your own journey of living with mental illness in your family. Share this book with others you know who walk this path. Thank you, Carole, for showing us how to face devastating life challenges and yet grow strong in Christ each step of the way."

—Chris Adams,
Speaker, Bible teacher, writer
Retired, Women's ministry specialist, LifeWay Christian Resources
Nashville, Tennessee

"Sometimes things occur in our lives that present problems or issues. And then there are times where the developments are so dire and unexpected, we feel crushed and unable to go on. How do we make our way through these obstacles of chaos and crisis? Carole Leathem has brought an outlook that can help many of us. In her book, Finding Joy in My Messy Life, she shows how one can face desperate circumstances without sacrificing love, faith, and joy. She illustrates that grace is not only something to experience, but also something to demonstrate. Though Carole never anticipated the manifestation of her husband's mental illness, and while the journey through the situation seemed inconceivable, her candid transparency in delivering this story brings encouragement and hope to those who may be dealing with fear concerning mental illness in their family. As she says in her book, there's a great difference between living in fear and living with fear. Mental illness has sometimes been tagged with a scarlet "M" in our minds, but Carole has brought a deeper understanding and acknowledgment of its reality. If you face these kinds of issues in your life, you will be encouraged and supported by Carole's honesty. While certainly not diminishing the confusion and devastation of dealing with her husband's circumstances, she shows how to strengthen your relationship with Jesus during adversity."

—Jeff Hood
Lead pastor, First Baptist Church, Fairfield, CA

"This book is for anyone who has a struggle that seems insurmountable. Carole shows us that finding joy is a process, and she lays it out step by step for us through her own experience. Whatever challenge, whatever mess you may find yourself in, Carole can help you. If you are living in circumstances that you think might ruin you, take heart: Carole's story of trusting God will inspire and empower you to choose joy and move forward in faith."

—Kimberly MacNeill
The Inspiration Lounge

"There are moments in life that cause us to come to a screeching halt. When life as we know it is turned upside down, and we are left with the decision to crumble in our brokenness and isolate from the world or to lean into the Lord and let Him start putting the pieces back together. It is in those moments we are reminded of how important it is to surround ourselves with those who will speak God's truth in our lives. In Carole's book, *Finding Joy in My Messy Life*, she transparently opens her life to give us an inside view of a woman and family faced with a crisis that so many families are facing in the dark by themselves. The subject of mental illness and suicidal thoughts is one that has been hidden far too long and needs to be brought to the light. We see through these pages one woman's journey of what it means to fully surrender those that we love the most to the Lord and how we can find joy in the journey when our trust is in Him alone. I have had the privilege of walking with Carole through most of this season. She has continued to live in the moment of putting one foot in front of the other and giving God the glory even on the darkest of days. None of us is promised tomorrow. While she would never have chosen this journey for her family, she has continued to share with all who will listen what God continues to teach her along the way. Learning to live a joy-filled life in the mess is possible, and she wants to take you on the journey with her. So, grab a cup of coffee, pull up a seat to her table, and let the words from these pages encourage your heart. Jesus tells us, 'I have told you these things, so that in me you may have peace. In this world you will have trouble. But take heart! I have overcome the world.' (John 16:33). Do not give up. We are in this together."

—Lynn Bradshaw, CA
Women's ministry director
Valley Baptist Church

"For more than four decades, I have called Bill and Carole my friends since our days as next-door neighbors in seminary. I laughed and cried my way through the raw, emotional, and turbulent roller-coaster ride of life upon which they continue to travel. This is a love story. It is a story of faith, trust, hope, and commitment. A story of courage—the willingness to bear the deep, dark secrets of the soul for all to see. As you read Bill and Carole's journey, you will realize that this is not a story about them at all. It is a story about God's incredible love and the gracious way in which He continues to speak into their lives."

—Glenn Prescott
Professor of Ministry Leadership
Gateway Seminary of the SBC
Ontario, California

*Finding Joy in My Messy Life* is a true-life story about author Carole Leathem's past five years of surviving her husband's mental battle with depression, anxiety, and suicidal thoughts. Carole, the eldest of four, gives great history about her upbringing. She speaks about her parents' marriage and divorce, her father abandoning the family, his verbal abuse specifically towards the mother and Carole, dealing with the negative effects of being fatherless, and moving forward to marrying her husband Bill. It is such a great read that I will not go into great detail. You must read it for yourself. However, I will say this: Carole's story reminds me of my mother's story. To make a long story short, my mother's parents got pregnant with my mother at the age of 14 and ended up marrying young. Like Carole's father and his struggle with being verbally abusive, my grandfather was sexually abusive and molested my mother in her early preteens. Like Carole, my mother had to overcome the struggles that came along with the abuse. You may ask, why do I mention Carole in relation to my mother? Carole's story of being fatherless, abused, hopeless, alone, and fearful gives her strength for the next chapter of her current situation. That chapter involves the mental health struggles of her husband Bill. No, it is not easy to deal with such a thing; however, Carole gives great detail in not giving up, researching, asking, looking, and constantly praying. Not many people are comfortable sharing their struggles. Why? Because of what others might say and how they will react. People can be very discouraging and negative. Carole shines a great light on her struggles to bring awareness and to help those who struggle with the same thing but do not have the courage to ask for help. *Finding Joy in My Messy Life* is inspiring, encouraging, and motivating. I pray this book opens your eyes to mental health and life struggles and gives you the tools to help fight it."

—Charlin Neal
Worship leader, vocal producer

"Twenty-plus years ago, Carole L., Carole C., and I were on our way home from an event, when I told Carole L. that God was going to use her to make a difference in the lives of many through her speaking and writing, after hearing her speak at a church event and reading her blogs. She has a way of bringing to life situations and circumstances that resonate and capture the heart of people. And it is this gift that God has and will use in Carole to bring an increased awareness to one of the most challenging healthcare conditions—mental health—in a way that will resonate and bring hope to many. In this book, *Finding Joy in my Messy Life*, Carole transparently shares Bill's and her trials, her imperfections, the messiness of various situations, her doubts and weaknesses and yet in the midst of it all, she shares how God's Holy Spirit has comforted her, directed her, and given her the strength to keep going onwards and upwards. She reveals how God met her in the eye of the storm of Bill's mental health condition and the various manifestations, how He is guiding her through this mental health turbulence, and how He is taking the messiness of her various experiences with Bill, family, friends and even adversaries to bring to life. Romans 8:28, "And we know that God causes everything to work together for the good of those who love God and are called according to his purpose for them." Through it all, Carole's love for God and hope in God shines through, even during the most difficult times. We pray that God uses this book, her speaking engagements, her ongoing blogs, and all that she does dealing with this and other challenging subjects, to bless and bring hope to many. And we pray that Carole will continue to be a reflection of God's love, grace, and mercy to all."

—Elizabeth Oyekan, PharmD, FCSHP, CPHQ
Vice President at Precision
CEO at Meds on a Mission
Author on leadership and healthcare topics

"*Finding Joy in My Messy Life* deals with a subject that many may not want to discuss or feel comfortable talking about—mental illness. Carole shares how she faces each day with her husband's anxiety, depression, and suicidal thoughts. With her transparency, she opens the door for people to understand how not only the person with mental illness, but their spouse, needs understanding, acceptance, and love. Carole has questions that many have: *Why is this happening to him, to us? I can't do this. I feel so helpless. Where are You, God?* Listen to her heart as she shares the answers God gave her and is giving her. Her dedication to God and her husband will inspire you to seek the most of your relationship. She uses everyday events to find answers to her questions by relating them to God's Word. Her perseverance will challenge many to seek help. This book will open your eyes to the need for helping others. To try to understand them in their time of need. It will also encourage you to stand with those you know and give them support, even if you may not know how. Carole's book gives insights into how to help the person and their spouse and family. *Finding Joy in My Messy Life* is not only a book to just read, but one to keep handy at a moment's notice."

—Charles C. Woods
Pastor, director of missions, author

"Within Christianity, there is often a lack of acknowledgment concerning mental illness; however, mental illness has no bias. It does not see culture, ethnicity, personality, appearances, intelligence, socio-economic background, skin color, religious affiliation, or occupation. Many have agonized in silence, and many more are experiencing anxiety, depression, and suicidal ideation as you read this. In her book, *Finding Joy in My Messy Life*, Carole Leathem has brought light to a dark subject within the church. Writing with extraordinary candor, she shares her personal experience regarding relationships, love, and life after her pastor husband was diagnosed with anxiety, depression, and suicidal ideation. Carole invites you into her 'messy' life by sharing her honest, transparent, and real-life struggles, as well as the truths she discovered about herself, mental illness, and her very real relationship with Jesus Christ."

National Suicide Prevention Hotline: (800) 273-8255

—Teresa Hood, MA
Registered Associate Marriage and Family Therapist
Children's pastor, First Baptist Church, Fairfield, CA

"One of the blights on the modern church is our stubbornness in addressing the mental health crisis—not just of our congregations, but of our clergy as well. Nearly every individual, couple, or family I counsel and serve has some level of depression, anxiety, or other mental health issue affecting their daily lives; this is not a rare or distant predicament, but rather the ever-present reality for so many of our brothers and sisters. This book is a bold, honest, and encouraging step in the right direction. Through this book, Carole is on the leading edge of openness and transparency in the struggles so many of us face. Her story is one of entrenched generational pain, persistent love in the face of daunting challenges, following God's call into uncharted waters, and ongoing victory in Christ. For these reasons and so many more, this book is for everyone who either loves someone struggling with mental health issues or seeks to be an agent of change in our deeply broken world."

—Ty Barksdale
Pastor, Valley Baptist Church

# Finding
# Joy
## IN MY MESSY LIFE

# Finding Joy

## IN MY MESSY LIFE

CAROLE LEATHEM

Published by Redemption Press, PO Box 427, Enumclaw, WA 98022.

Toll-Free (844) 2REDEEM (273-3336)

Redemption Press is honored to present this title in partnership with the author. The views expressed or implied in this work are those of the author. Redemption Press provides our imprint seal representing design excellence, creative content, and high quality production.

ISBN 13: 978-1-64645-259-0 (Paperback)
978-1-64645-260-6 (ePub)
978-1-64645-261-3 (Mobi)

Library of Congress Catalog Card Number: 2020923444

To Bill—
I handed you my whole heart the moment I saw you,
and God whispered,
*There he is, that's your husband.*
Love is about facing everything together.
We are finding joy in our messy life by holding on to God
and loving each other,
even when things don't turn out as we plan.
Life is an adventure, and I am happy to share every moment
of my journey with you.
I fell in love with you the moment I met you.
I have loved you every moment since.
I will love you every moment we have yet to live.

*Consider it a sheer gift, friends,*
*when tests and challenges come at you from all sides.*
*You know that under pressure, your faith-life is forced into the open*
*and shows its true colors.*
*So don't try to get out of anything prematurely.*
*Let it do its work so you become mature and well-developed,*
*not deficient in any way.*
*If you don't know what you're doing, pray to the Father.*
*He loves to help.*
*You'll get his help, and won't be condescended to when you ask for it.*
*Ask boldly, believingly, without a second thought.*

James 1:2–5

# Contents

Foreword by Bill Leathem     17

Acknowledgments     19

Introduction     23

Chapter 1:   How Could This Happen to Bill?     33

Chapter 2:   Why Is This Happening?     45

Chapter 3:   Facing Emotional Tumbleweeds     55

Chapter 4:   The Source of My Strength, Power, and Joy     63

Chapter 5:   The Difference between Living in Fear and Living with It     73

Chapter 6:   Facing the Opposition That Comes with Obedience     85

Chapter 7:   God's Gift to Us Is in the Trials     93

Chapter 8:   Mastering Mental Gymnastics     103

Chapter 9:   Learning to Live with What I Have     113

Chapter 10: Leaning into God and His Truths     121

Chapter 11: When It's Time to Reset     129

Chapter 12: Knee Deep in Joy     139

Carole's Survival Tips and Tools     149

# Foreword

Let me start out by saying, I have read the manuscript, and I am supportive of Carole in sharing our story. Neither of us knew that the events that occurred in 2015 were going to challenge us as the greatest trauma in our life together. We had no idea the depth of confusion that would occur for both of us when I began to suffer from anxiety, depression, and suicidal thoughts.

Throughout much of our marriage, Carole has been a motivating speaker, impactful leader, inspired risk taker, and encouraging storyteller. She has always been open about her faith in God and the challenges in her life, beginning with her early years and being abandoned by an abusive alcoholic father. She has continued this transparency by sharing about the painful journey we have walked through these past five years together. She felt led by God to put our story in print, so I encourage her in the hope that her openness, transparency, and honesty will help those who read it.

Carole and I are both committed to the truth that we are partners for life and that our common faith in God will empower us to work our way through life together. A commitment to our faith and to respecting our uniqueness has been the foundation for our relationship. I have always said, "I want to get to the end of my life with a real faith and a blessed marriage," and that is what has been happening for forty-four years with Carole.

I pray that this book will be a source of encouragement to you, especially if you are on a similar journey. As you read our story in *Finding Joy in My Messy Life*, enjoy Carole's unique style of storytelling, inspired thoughts, and sometimes painful recollections of our journey.

I love you, sweetie.

Bill

# Acknowledgments

When God began talking to me about writing this book, I told Him, *I can't—the story isn't finished.* But God knows that if I wait until my mess is over, the book may never get written. He said, *Don't wait—do it now.* So I began writing, and the next week I got a call from a woman whose son had tried to commit suicide. She knew I was writing a book on this subject, and she said, "Will you please finish that book? I really need it now." There are so many of us with loved ones who struggle with mental illness.

I have been blessed to have many cheerleaders encouraging me, praying for me, and holding me accountable to finish this book. I thank God for each one of you.

To those I love who have lost someone to suicide—God knows your pain, and I pray for you daily.

To those I love who care for someone struggling with mental illness—we are in this together. God sees you, and I see you.

To my family—Bill, Kate, Luke, Jack, LeeAnn, Tyson, Kinslee, Henry, CJ, Liam, and Brenlee—I love you all so much. You have been my biggest cheerleaders and encouragers in life. The thought of each of you brings a smile to my face and warms my heart. I have loved all of our Disney adventures, and I can't wait for the next one.

For my mom, Dottie—even in your own mess, you made sure I had a stable foundation in God so I would be prepared years later to live through my own chaos. I love you.

To my siblings, John, Trish, and Stephen—we have had so many adventures tricycles, eggs, and party-line phones. John, I am sorry for the scar on your arm. Trish, you are still my favorite birthday gift. Stephen, you will always be my baby.

To Sandy—we may not be sisters by blood, but we are sisters by choice. I love you.

To Lynn, *my valley girls*, and the gals from Joy Filled Women—when people find out I choose to live in Bakersfield, they look at me like I am crazy. They have no idea the incredible group of God's girls who live here. I am not crazy; I am blessed beyond measure to have each of you in my life.

To Steve and Peggy—thank you for modeling what a godly family looks like.

To Matt—you were a handful when I babysat you, but I love God's sense of humor. Thank you for mentoring my son in ministry.

To Deryl and Brenda—I don't even know where to begin, so I will simply say, *thank you!*

To Elizabeth, Carole, Nancy, Tammy, Kimberly, and Diane—God knew I would need each of you to help me survive these past five years, so He sent you to me years ago. Thanks for being willing to love me, cry with me, and pray for me. I love each of you dearly.

To Pastor Roger—thank you for pointing me to the Bible and to God every week.

To Pastor Andrew—thank you for being obedient. One morning you stood from the stage and said, "I don't know who needs to hear this verse today, but here it is." You quoted my life verse, Proverbs 3:5–6, and reminded me where my strength comes from. That morning I was in crisis and at a breaking point.

To Athena, Dori, Hannah, and the team at Redemption Press—thank you for your encouragement, hard work, and support in getting my book published. To Jennifer, my writing coach—God knew exactly who I needed to help me; I have loved working with you.

To my number one fan, Tami—thank you for encouraging me by being the first to step up and buy my book and support me.

To Kelly—when you looked at me and said, "Will you please get that book done? I need it," God was speaking to me through your words.

To Tami, Sharilyn, Eva, Melissa, Beverly, Teresa, Greg, Stacie, Lela, Wichian, Jane, Erin, Susan, Erika, John, Dottie, Carlanne, Renee, Kimberly, Alberta, Chanh, Diane, Deb, June, Stella, Leslie, Kathy, Linda, Theresa, Judy, Veronica, Janet, Carla, Kimberly, Vince, Norna, Cynthia, Gayle, Nancy, Serena, Donna, Janet, Marcy, Gary, Nancy, Beverly, Susan, Joyce, Sandy, Sharon, Sophie, Joyce, DeLynn, Tina, Nancy, Loralyn, Lisa, Tamara, Trish, Debbie, Cherie, Vickie, Janelle, Tonya, and Sheryl—you have blessed me by preordering the book and financially supporting me. Thank you!

# Introduction

*Life can only be understood backwards;*
*but it must be lived forwards.*

—Søren Aabye Kierkegaard

When I find something that speaks to me, I write it on a sticky note and hang it on my window. This quote by Søren Aabye Kierkegaard is posted right in the middle of my window, and I read it often. As a sixteen-year-old, if I had known the path my life would take, I'm pretty sure I would have sat down like a mule and refused to take one more step. At that time in my life, I had come to know Christ and had a newfound knowledge about the direction I wanted to steer my life toward. It was impossible to go back and alter my childhood experiences, but I found myself full of hope, living forward, and dragging trunks filled with hurts, fears, regrets, anger, and rejection with me.

What is your earliest childhood memory? Mine is hearing my dad's car pull into the driveway and me running to the refrigerator to grab a can of beer to greet him with at the door. He would pop the tab, take a drink, and pat my head. If it was a good night, after dinner he would drop to the couch and fall asleep watching TV. If it was a bad night, something or someone, usually me, would set off his terrifying rage.

I used to stand at the living room window and watch the neighbor's dad come home from work. His kids would run to his car in the driveway, and he would pick them up, smile at them, and give them a big hug. I would stand there, my eyes glued to the scene, until he grabbed the hands of each of the two kids and walked into the house. I imagined the love, laughter, and hugs those kids got. I wanted that family and their dad and his smiles and hugs. I have no memory of my dad ever touching me unless it was the back of his hand connecting with whatever part of my body he could reach at the moment.

Our family attended church regularly on Sundays, where you would see my beautiful, smart mother and my fun-loving, life-of-the-party father. We appeared to be the perfect family, yet appearances can be a dangerous illusion. Nobody knew that behind closed doors my father was a monster. My idyllic family life ended the moment the front doors of our house closed and my father's rage erupted. I learned from a very young age that the more beer my dad drank, the less of a chance his rage would turn physical.

I once asked my grandmother why my dad was so mad all the time. She said, "Carole Lee, your daddy is a wonderful father. What are you talking about?" I learned from the experience with my grandmother that my father was a chameleon who could turn on the charm and dazzle anyone he came into contact with. My mom and I were the only ones to experience the consuming anger lurking inside him. When I look back on my childhood, I see now that I used imagination to create stories that would instantly take me away from all the pain and rejection I faced from having an abusive and alcoholic father. My silly stories, imaginary friends, and make-believe pets would irritate him into a rage of screaming, hitting, and throwing things. I wanted to be invisible like my friends.

As my three siblings arrived, life got even more chaotic. Coming home to four active children after a long day at work was more than my dad could handle. His drinking and rage escalated to the point where he could no longer keep a job. As the oldest child, I became the self-appointed caretaker. The day my mom brought my youngest brother home from the hospital, she put him in my arms, and he became my baby. He slept in a crib in my room, and I hovered over him constantly. My mom had to work because my dad couldn't, and that meant I was often left in charge. I fell easily into the mother role. I was nine and I had a perfect little family . . . my brother who was seven, my sister four, and the baby. I became responsible for most of the cooking and cleaning. I also became a fierce protector, always putting myself between my siblings and my dad when he was in a rage. When our parents fought, I would gather the children into my bedroom and tuck the kids into my bed while I lay down on the floor in front of the closed door.

When I was eleven, my dad went on a "vacation" and never came back. The day I realized he was not coming back brought a combination of relief and guilt. Being the oldest, I believed somehow it was my fault he left. I had nightmares about what I had done to make him leave and kept asking myself if I could have done something to make him stay. Issues of abandonment and rejection became firmly cemented into my identity.

When he left, he really left, meaning no phone calls, no visits, and no birthday or Christmas gifts. He didn't help my mom financially. He simply disappeared. My mom became a divorcee at a time when the church didn't accept divorce. She was single with four children to support and trying to figure out who she was. We were the original latchkey kids left on our own far too often. Because I felt like it was my fault our dad left, I took on even more responsibility for the family.

My mom made it a priority to keep us in church. This was hard for her because the people in the church were judgmental of our family. Divorce was not common then and was considered a huge sin. As the children of the divorcee, we also felt the judgment of the church members. When I was twelve, my Sunday school teacher was teaching on the Ten Commandments from Exodus 20. When she got to the words in verse 5 warning of "punishing the children for any sins their parents pass on to them," she looked right at me. In front of the class, she said, "See, God punishes the children for their parents' sin. You are hopeless. You will grow up and get divorced too."

The judgment I received was not just reserved for the people of the church; people outside the church joined in too. I was responsible for getting the two youngest children to school every morning before I caught the bus to my junior high school. As I was dropping my youngest brother off at his classroom one day, his teacher said to me, with sarcasm and eye rolls, in front of the other parents, "We are putting together the Thanksgiving basket for this year's needy family, and your family always gets it. So this year we decided to ask you what you will actually eat so it doesn't go to waste." I was completely embarrassed. I found out later that my brother's teacher from the year before had asked him if he enjoyed his basket of food. He had told her that our family hated green beans and pumpkin pie, so we had thrown them in the trash. This was not true.

I put so much pressure on myself to care for my family that by the age of fourteen, I had ulcers and just wanted out. Not only did I have more responsibility than a teenager should have to carry—caring for my siblings and the food and the house—but I also had the burden of the responsibility without the authority. As my siblings got older, they realized they didn't have to listen to me because I was not their mom. By the age of sixteen, I found myself tired, hopeless, rejected, and feeling like that was all I deserved.

I was dating a guy just like my father. We had started going to church together, and he was the life of the party. People told me how lucky I was to have such a great boyfriend. No one knew what he was really like when no one else was around. He drank, experimented with drugs, and was verbally abusive to me. The cycle was starting all over again, but I was convinced this was all I deserved. I stopped being the mom at home, gave up on school, and just wanted out.

I was ready to run away and get married because I believed no one else would love me. It was hopeless.

Despite all that, I attended church every Sunday. I was active in the youth group, but I didn't pay attention. I went because it was the one place no one expected anything of me. I was invisible. No cooking or cleaning or other responsibilities—I could just be left alone. I wanted nothing to do with God. I had heard people describe God as a father, and I knew from experience how a father would let me down. I was having none of it. I had been taught that God punished you for your parents' sins, and I knew this was unfair, so I didn't want to know God. I went to church for one reason and one reason only—to get away from my hopeless life. I am so glad that I kept going because one Sunday night, God started talking to me and I started listening.

I was sitting in church on the back pew with my guinea pig in my lap. I was doing my math homework, and I could hear the pastor speaking, but I was not paying attention to anything he was saying. All of a sudden, I heard these words very clearly, "Do you know that God loves you just the way you are? Do you know that there is nothing you have ever done, or will do, that will make Him stop loving you?" I looked up at my friend sitting next to me and whispered, "What did he say?" As my question left my lips, I heard the pastor reply, "I said, 'Do you know that God loves you just the way you are? Do you know that there is nothing you have ever done, or will do, that will make Him stop loving you?'" He finished by saying, "When are you going to stop running away from Jesus and give Him your life? He has a plan for your life that only you can fulfill, and it can start right now." I knew my life was a hopeless mess, and if I didn't change courses, it was about to get even messier. I was desperate. I wanted a real family. I wanted to be loved. I wanted to know I was important to someone. I wanted hope.

The word *hope* is defined as, "a person or thing that may help or save someone."[1] I was a girl desperately in need of being rescued.

I had never heard God described this way before, and at that moment, I decided He was my only hope. I wanted to know this God.

Our church always gave an invitation at the end of the sermon, and as the pastor started to pray, I handed my guinea pig to my friend and ran down the aisle. I stood in front of him, crying and barefoot and one big mess, when he opened his eyes. I could tell he was surprised. I said to him, "I just gave my life to Jesus. What do I do next? I want Jesus to break the cycle of abuse and addiction that has plagued my family for years." He stared at me, then handed me quickly off to a woman standing behind me. She took me in a backroom and asked me to pray this prayer. I told her I had already given my life to Jesus, so what was next? She kept repeating I had to pray the prayer. Finally I gave in and repeated the words after her. It was kind of comical—she had her eyes closed and mine were open, staring at her. As soon as she said, "Amen," the next words out of my mouth were, "Now what do I do?" Her answer to my question was to escort me back to the pastor. My first words to him were, "Now what do I do?" He looked a bit overwhelmed at my enthusiasm and told me to call the office the next morning and make an appointment to talk about baptism. I was excited, I had hope, and I was ready to take on the world because I now knew Jesus, and He loved me just the way I was. In that moment, the course of my life was forever changed.

That next week I sat in the pastor's office talking to him about getting baptized and my new journey with God. I will forever be grateful to Pastor Richard. With one question he helped me determine my first step in breaking the cycle. He asked me, "Do you love your boyfriend?" I said, "No, but there is no one else." I began to describe our relationship in detail. I told him about the drinking, drugs, and verbal abuse. He didn't judge me, and he gave me hope when he said, "God has a plan for your life. He has someone special for you, someone who will love you. You need to start praying that God will show you who that person is. He will make it very clear when you meet him."

After much discussion, I decided my first action was to break up with my boyfriend. I left the pastor's office that day and drove home. Later that same afternoon as I babysat my neighbor's children, my boyfriend called their house. We were supposed to go out that night, and he wanted to know what time to pick me up. I told him, "You're not picking me up, and I don't want to see you anymore. God has someone better for me—someone who loves Jesus as much as I do." So after two years of dating, I broke up with him because Jesus wanted me to. He hung up on me without saying anything.

I began reading and studying the Bible. I started to learn about God and grow in my understanding of who He is. God put three women and two men in my life that year. Peggy, Eileen, and Dawn mentored me. These women loved me, listened to me, prayed for me, and guided me. Pastor Richard and Pastor Steve taught me the Bible and how to apply it to my life. These men modeled for me what a godly man acted like. Steve and Peggy treated me like family. I spent time in their home babysitting their two boys, and I got to see firsthand how a godly mom and dad raised their kids. I remember telling myself all those years ago that I was going to raise my children like they did.

Have you ever wondered if God has a sense of humor? He does. As I write these words, my son, Jack, serves in ministry with one of those two boys I babysat. Steve and Peggy's youngest son, Matt, became a pastor and started a church. That church now has multiple locations and thousands of members. My son is on staff as the campus pastor for one of the locations. I am watching this boy I babysat, now a pastor, mentor my son who is now a pastor in his ministry. It's funny how life works.

As I continued to live my life forward, I managed to drag my trunks of pain and disappointment with me. I met my husband, Bill, during my senior year in high school. We married after I graduated, and he began to help me understand and heal from the hurts, fears, regrets, anger, and rejection I carried into our marriage. He loved me, taught me about letting go of the stuff in the trunks, and showed me that a husband and father can be committed and stay. Even as I was learning to trust, my greatest fear became that Bill would reject me one day. It took me thirty-nine years to finally let go of that fear. I had finally learned to trust him. I learned this just in time to walk through the darkest and scariest time of my life.

In 2015 the words, "My husband struggles with anxiety, depression, and suicidal thoughts," became the hardest words I had ever spoken out loud. We didn't see it coming, and it derailed our lives. I began to search for practical help in dealing with his mood swings, outbursts of anger, blame, paranoia, and withdrawal. I found none. I reached out to people I knew in the medical and religious communities, but no one had any help to offer. I wanted to find that person who had answers for me, but no one had any answers. I felt totally abandoned and alone. Fortunately I am stubborn and didn't give up. I kept reading everything I could find, asking questions, developing practical ways to survive, and most of all, trusting God.

One day a friend said to me, "Tell them! Stop searching for answers and start writing about what you have learned and how you survive." I believe that our lives are a journey. As our paths cross, we become a part of one another's journey. It is not an accident you are holding this book and reading these pages. God has a plan for all of us. Our lives for this moment are on the same path. Maybe your life is a mess, maybe not. If your life is a mess, I am right there with you. If your life is not a mess right now, those of us in a mess need you. We need you to be there for us. We need your strength to encourage us, to hug us, to sit quietly with us. We need you to point us to God so we can find joy in our messy lives. For me, the months have turned into years, and we still have no answers—no real solutions or resolution. But I do have joy, and that's what I want for you too.

If you relate to my story in even a small way, I want you to know you are not alone. God sees you and I see you. The journey will be daunting and overwhelming, so take a deep breath, focus for a moment on something that makes you smile, and keep going. You can do this; we can do this together.

As you read the following pages, I am going to share with you the biblical and practical coping tools I use daily to survive. I like to joke and say that I am God's favorite daughter because He just keeps showing up and taking care of me. The truth is He loves us all, and we are all His favorites. He will show up for you in the same way He has for me. My life is still one big mess, and I live every moment finding joy in my messy life. So can you.

# 1

## How Could This Happen to Bill?

*Just because you don't understand it doesn't mean it isn't so.*
—Lemony Snicket

From the moment I saw him, I knew he was my person. I was seventeen years old and sitting on the front row in my church's worship center. I turned and looked toward the back of the room as he walked in. I heard God say, *There he is, that's your husband.* I turned to my friend, Teri, sitting next to me and said, "I am going to marry that guy." We were introduced by mutual friends that day, and a few weeks later, Bill invited me on a midnight motorcycle ride. That night we decided to begin dating, and I started to plan my fairytale wedding. We were married fifteen months later and vowed to love each other in sickness or health, for richer or poorer, until death parts us.

I was eighteen years old when I married Bill—just seven months out of high school. I had been raised by an abusive, alcoholic father who abandoned me when I was eleven. My mother was enjoying the single life of partying and dating in the seventies, and I had become mom to her and my three siblings. I had no example to follow of a working marriage; I just knew that divorce was not an option for me. I believed God planned my marriage to Bill. I was committed and in it for life. I didn't need to worry because Bill was dependable, strong, hardworking, and committed to God and family. He was nothing like my father and would never leave me or reject me.

Whenever I have a moment where I feel like I can't go on and want to quit, I go back and remember that day and God's words: *There he is, that's your husband.* The memory keeps me going, but it also sets the stage for the question: how could this happen to my strong, dependable Bill? It's the same question everyone who ever knew him would one day ask.

Early in our dating relationship, I began to notice something different about Bill. When he got upset about something, he had a hard time letting it go. If he got angry or upset with me, he would push me verbally until he felt there was a resolution. He was so worried about my family background of divorce that he struggled asking me to marry him. He wanted me to commit to not getting a divorce before I even committed to marrying him.

In our first year of marriage, I experienced moments when his anxiety was so high he even acted it out in his dreams. We lived in Citrus Heights, California, and our apartment was located in an area that was being terrorized by the East Area Rapist. Bill was so anxious and fearful that he placed a board under our bedroom door every night. One night his anxiety caused him to have a nightmare, and he began to act it out. He sat straight up in bed, and in his sleep he reached over and shoved me off the bed to the floor. As I was trying to wake up and wiggle myself out of the crevice between the bed and the wall, I heard him begin screaming at the doorway, "Stop right where you are; stay away." It took me a few seconds to realize he was dreaming. I crawled back up on the bed and began trying to wake him up. He never did wake up. Still sleeping he looked at me with wild eyes, gently pushed me back down on my pillow and said, "It's okay, he is gone; go back to sleep." I lay there in the dark, adrenaline pumping, wondering what just happened. The next morning when I asked him about it, he had no memory of it.

I also noticed that when a change needed to happen, he pushed until it was resolved and had an extreme need to control everything. While he thought he was being helpful, his behavior came across as negative and controlling. I am a creative, fluid person who fights against routine, so this was really hard for me. In his defense, we were living on a really tight budget, and I routinely spent more than our grocery budget would allow. I refused to track the costs. I just knew I needed those tomatoes, radishes, and mushrooms for my salads, even if it meant going over the weekly budget. I also struggled to get the house cleaned and laundry done, *in a timely fashion*, as Bill called it. He would make lists and schedules for me and then would say, "Just follow the list and schedule. Do the cleaning and laundry on these days at these times. Don't let anything get in the way." I, on the other hand, would forget to look at the lists and schedules, lose them, or simply ignore them if something came up that was more fun, like lunch with a friend. For example, one Monday morning, my schedule read, "Clean the bathroom at 10 a.m." Well at 9:55 a.m., a friend called. We talked on the phone for an hour, and after we hung up, I forgot to clean. When Bill came home from work, he was so upset he kicked a plant across the room.

He had also determined while we were dating that I didn't understand style and color, which explained why I couldn't pick out the right kind of clothing. After our marriage, we both worked in retail so he would routinely come home with clothes and shoes that he'd describe as "perfect for me." Somewhere along the way he even began to determine who my friends should be. His rationale was: "I am helping you avoid messy relationships by picking the wrong friends."

By year two of our marriage, we had moved to the San Francisco Bay Area so Bill could attend seminary. I worked full time so Bill could go to school. His control and negativity were hard to deal with. On our second anniversary, he gave in to my constant bugging, and we went to Hawaii. The entire plane trip he kept looking at me and saying, "I have no idea why I let you talk me into this. We have perfectly good beaches at home without this expense and trouble." To my excitement, Bill fell in love with Hawaii on that first trip. He became familiar with the weather, environment, and culture and this brought comfort. His comfort engaged his need for control, which meant after that trip, I couldn't get him to travel anywhere else. We have currently been to the islands more than forty times.

When he finished his seminary degree three years later, we began to interview for positions in church ministry. It is common for the wife to be included in the interviews. Bill would attempt to preplan my answers to questions he thought I would be asked. This brought more to worry about and more attempts to control. The church is full of people with opinions and needs. He tried to juggle it all. I remember after an interview with a church's search committee, we received a letter saying we were rejected because I wore designer jeans to the meeting. Bill tried working as a music and youth minister, then he tried to plant a church, but nothing seemed to work. Finally God opened the door for him to become a senior pastor and his response was, "Good, when this doesn't work either, I will leave ministry."

We had been married for eight years when he started his first position as a senior pastor, and this brought new pressure on both of us. Growing up with an abusive, alcoholic father, my greatest fear was rejection. I soon discovered that I couldn't please some of the women in our church. They had expectations of their new pastor's wife, and I was routinely rejected and publicly criticized. I couldn't play the piano. I didn't want to work in the nursery. I didn't sing solos or even sing in the choir. To get back at me, the women placed my name on the schedule for the nursery every month. I fought back by not showing up. During a church talent show, I was assigned a piano solo in the printed program, so I played chopsticks. As the pressure got to me, it also was getting to Bill. He began to turn on me as well and became more controlling and negative. I couldn't do anything right, and I felt like I was becoming everyone's problem.

Life became more complicated when our two children were born—now there were two more people for him to worry about and try to control. Have you ever tried to control an infant and a fourteen-month-old at the same time? I was also beginning to fight back against the control. I wanted to pick my friends, and then go out to dinner, a movie, or go shopping with them. I wanted to pick out my own clothing. I felt like a rebellious teenager.

We moved to Santa Clarita in 1990, and Bill became the pastor of a small, struggling church. As soon as we moved, doors began to open for me to work in Hollywood as a commercial actress. I landed an agent, and I loved my new life and career. Bill was supportive of me, yet under the surface he was about to implode. The pressure, anxiety, and lack of control where I was concerned, structural building problems with the church, and trying to control and please everyone in the congregation began taking a toll on him. I began wondering what was happening to him.

In 1992, we celebrated our fifteenth wedding anniversary. At the time, he had been the pastor of a church in Newhall, California, for two years. He was thirty-eight, and his anxiety, need for control, and rumination got so bad that he experienced his first emotional breakdown. This was the first time I found myself asking how this could happen to Bill, as I stood in a hospital corridor at 2:30 in the morning, waiting for a nurse to take me to see him. A few hours earlier, I had found him lying on the floor of our living room in tears holding his chest. I called 911 and a deacon from our church and then sat down next to him on the floor to wait. Sobbing, he told me, "I'm having a heart attack." As I sat stroking his forehead, I began to suspect that his problem had nothing to do with his heart.

The ambulance arrived, and the paramedics began asking him questions, "Are you dizzy?" "Does this hurt?" "Is your chest feeling tight?" They took his blood pressure and listened to his heart. After a few minutes I could see them relax a tiny bit, as there were no signs of a heart attack. They determined that he should go to the hospital to be checked out. The deacon and his wife arrived as Bill was being loaded into the ambulance. The medics told me where they were taking Bill and that I should meet them at the hospital. Our children—Kate, seven, and Jack, five—were asleep upstairs, so the deacon's wife stayed with them while he drove me to the hospital.

As I stood in the hallway of the emergency room waiting for the nurse, the question kept repeating in my mind: *How did this happen to Bill?* The nurse arrived and led me to the room where Bill was being examined by a doctor. As I walked in, I heard the doctor say, "Pastor, I have seen this before; you guys forget you're not God and take responsibility for everything. You are not handling your stress, and you are trying to control the world." He then told Bill he wanted to prescribe a medication to help him, but Bill immediately said, "No, I can calm down on my own." The doctor then asked me to join him in the hallway and told me that Bill was suffering from severe anxiety and that we needed to find him a counselor as soon as possible. He also let me know that Bill would benefit from medication. My suspicions were correct . . . this had nothing to do with his heart.

I brought Bill home from the hospital the next day, and we soon found a counselor for him. After a few months of counseling, he seemed to calm down and he was back at work. I didn't yet understand, however, that mental illness is a cycle. I didn't see that the cycle was starting over as he went right back to his anxiety and controlling ways.

Following this first breakdown, I had my first experience with the discomfort others experience when dealing with mental illness. The members in our church didn't want to talk openly about what had happened to their pastor. He was supposed to be strong and close to God, a rock everyone could depend on. A few of the church members began whispering the question behind our backs, "How could this happen to Bill?" Bill explained it away as stress and assured everyone he was getting help. I felt like everyone, including Bill, was simply sweeping it under a rug, and they felt more comfortable ignoring the issues and pretending nothing had happened.

Several years later, the pressure started to get to Bill again. The cycle was repeating itself. He couldn't handle the daily and weekly responsibility of pastoring a church. His anger and anxiety flashed daily. His favorite task of preparing a sermon each week was now so much pressure that he wanted out. Our daughter was getting ready to graduate from high school, and we had a family trip planned, a two-week trip to Maui to celebrate. Bill informed me that when we got back from Hawaii, he was going to quit his job.

When we arrived home from the vacation, he did just that, and God opened the door for Bill to make a career change. He went from being a pastor to working for a foundation and helping churches raise money to build buildings. The pressure seemed gone, and his job appeared to be a perfect fit for his abilities and personality.

A year later we moved to Fresno and built a beautiful house. We had nice cars, more money than we could spend in a month, and great friends. From the outside, our lives looked perfect. No one could see how miserable I was. I could tell from watching Bill that he was about to fall apart again, and everyone kept telling us how lucky and blessed we were. The cycle of anxiety, control, and emotional breakdowns continued. He would seem okay for a while, and then the cycle would start all over again. He would turn on me with his control and negativity and then end up in the hospital thinking he was having a heart attack. The doctors would tell him, "You're not handling your stress. You need counseling and medication." And again Bill would say, "I can calm down on my own."

Our world began to slowly and silently crumble. We had been living in Fresno for three years, and Bill realized that working for the organization gave him less input than he had anticipated. This began to mess once again with his control issues. He had another emotional breakdown because of the anxiety and lack of control. He couldn't eat or sleep, and he cried all the time. The economy crashed, and the organization he was working for was in financial trouble. They began to let people go, and Bill was let go in the first round of job cuts. We had enough money in savings, so we didn't panic. Bill decided it was time to go back to working in the local church as a pastor. We began to search for what would be next. What neither of us knew was that his body and emotions were beginning to break under the strain. As he got weaker, he couldn't handle stress of any kind. If his leadership was questioned, he became angry and pushy. Meanwhile I was getting emotionally stronger and learning to stand up for myself and become more decisive. Things began to shift in the household, and I began to manage our money, speak up, make decisions, and even pick my own friends and clothing. The shift was so subtle that I didn't even see it happening.

After a year of searching for a job, we ended up right back where we had started eight years before—the same city, the same church, the same people, the same problems. This time it was temporary. We knew that we would be in Newhall, California, for about two years to help the church get financially stable and to find another pastor. We moved into a small apartment because we now had less stuff and less money.

Bill was miserable. His anxiety and need to control were out of control. He made comments to people that were out of character and created problems. People in leadership of the church were beginning to see his anger and control issues in decisions he made. During a four-week period of time, he had health issues, such as a hernia repair surgery and an emergency appendectomy with major complications and infection. I began to see how his mind and body were suffering from the pressure of his anxiety. I watched helplessly as my husband was imploding, and I couldn't stop it. The Newhall church finally became stable, and they called a new pastor. It was time for us to leave, and we relocated to pastor a church in Fairfield, California. Little did we know that this move would be the one that created the perfect storm of emotional chaos that would permanently change the landscape of our lives.

The storm started as soon as we moved to Fairfield, which was experiencing a housing boom. It took six months for us to find and purchase a home, and we lived in a small hotel room for those six months. We made offers on ten homes and were overbid. When we finally purchased our home, the night before the sale was to close, the sellers refused to sign. It was frustrating, and it took ten days to convince them to close the deal. We had a vacation planned to Hawaii, so we left all our possessions in a car in our realtor's garage. Bill couldn't relax on our vacation and was constantly checking his cell phone, email, and voice messages. The house finally closed the day we flew home, and we started to get settled.

I loved our life in Fairfield. We had a great church and a beautiful home. We had recovered financially from the economic crash, and I thought we were enjoying the pace of life. But a few months later, Bill's anxiety and need for control came back with a vengeance. I started to notice he was more agitated, got frustrated more easily, and couldn't handle stress. Then his blood pressure started slowly creeping up higher and higher. His doctor wanted to put him on blood pressure medication, but he refused. He became pushy and opinionated about everything I did. Bill was miserable, and I had no idea how to help him. I was stronger and more secure than I had ever been and fought back against being controlled.

As I continued to fight against the control, Bill got angrier and pushed me harder. I found myself tiptoeing around an emotional minefield, never knowing when my words or actions would set him off on an angry tirade. I found myself often wondering why he was so mad at me. In hindsight, I was able to understand what was going on.

On a sunny October afternoon, God told me that we were going to move to Bakersfield, California. My daughter lived there, and we were visiting her for a few days. I was reading the newspaper one morning and saw an ad for some model homes called NextGen Homes. They had small apartments attached to the main house, making it convenient for families to live together. I was intrigued and felt like we should go look at them. That afternoon Bill and I took a drive to get out of the house. I told him I wanted to go look at the model homes I'd seen in the paper, but he was not very nice and said, "This is a waste of time. I will *never* live in Bakersfield, especially if it means living with Kate and her family." We went anyway and found the model homes. As we toured one that had an attached apartment, I walked into the bedroom and heard God say, *You are moving here soon and will live in a house like this here in Bakersfield. Get ready, Carole, a mess and a huge change is coming.* I realized that if something ever happened to Bill, this is exactly where I would want to be. I put the brochure in my purse as we walked out.

A few weeks later, Bill's doctor was unavailable for his check up, and we had to see another doctor. After talking to Bill for a few minutes and looking over his chart, she stared at him and said, "I know exactly what is wrong with you. My husband is a retired pastor, and I have seen the same issues in him. You can no longer manage the stress of your job; you need to retire."

The next day we took a drive up to the mountains, and I asked Bill, "What would it look like to retire. Could we manage?" We decided to check out some options, the first being the possibility of selling our home. I called Karan, a realtor in our church. I needed to tell her something, so I told her that Bill and I were preparing for retirement someday in Bakersfield. I told her that upon retirement we wanted to move into a home we found with an attached two-bedroom apartment, sell our home now, and rent an apartment in Fairfield until Bill was ready to retire. We wanted to buy the house with our daughter now so that Kate and her family could go ahead and move in, and we would move sometime in the future. Karan told me we were wise to think about the future and that she would love to have the same opportunity with her daughter.

We made an appointment for Karan to come over the next Tuesday to look at our house and talk about options for selling it. As I hung up, Bill looked at me and said, "That is exactly what we are going to do, isn't it?" I said, "Yes, it is." The realtor came the next week, and in an incredible series of God-orchestrated events, we sold our home for a full-price, cash offer, bought the one God told me we would live in, in Bakersfield—all over the next seven weeks. We closed escrow on December 29, 2015, and then we decided not to move into an apartment. It was time to set a retirement date and we did, for January 31, 2016. Bill's blood pressure dropped to a normal range that day. I thought we were out of the woods.

The same day that Bill's blood pressure dropped, he got a call from a man named Ralph. Ralph was the chairman of a search committee for a church in Sacramento and wanted Bill to give him a reference on a fellow they were interviewing for a temporary, executive pastor position. Bill knew Ralph from his days working in Fresno at the foundation. As they talked, Bill shared with Ralph about our move and his retirement date. Ralph and Bill began to talk about Bill taking the part-time position as soon as he retired, instead of the guy they were interviewing. Bill expressed to me that this was his dream retirement job. I questioned him, "We haven't even retired yet, and you want to go back to work?" I was frustrated, even though the position took us back home to Sacramento, to the church where I grew up, to the church where I met God, to the church where I met and married Bill. There were even a few people still in the church who had been there all those years ago.

As soon as Bill retired, we began commuting from Bakersfield to Sacramento every week. We would spend four days working with the church, stay three nights in a hotel, then drive back to our home in Bakersfield for three days. The drive took five hours one way, and within a few weeks, Bill began to develop anxiety about driving. His anxiety got so bad he could no longer drive, and I had to do all the driving. Then he began to need me to be with him everywhere. I had to be with him at the church, or if I couldn't be there in person, I was on the phone with him constantly.

By September 2016, Bill was developing depression, and things were getting out of control. I was the only one who knew of the chaos and of the mess we were dealing with. By October the depression and anxiety had completely taken over Bill's mind. He couldn't sleep, and I forced him to eat. I took him to doctor after doctor, and no one seemed to be able to help him. Finally, suicidal thoughts joined the anxiety and depression, and my husband no longer wanted to be alive.

How could this happen to Bill? How did it get this far? I still have no answers to these questions, even now.

# 2

## Why Is This Happening?

*Asking "Why" can lead to understanding.*
*Asking "Why not?" can lead to breakthrough.*
—Daniel H. Pink

**For most of 2016, I had been living with a nagging feeling** that something was not right. We had been retired for almost a year and were visiting our son and his wife for the month of November, helping out with our grandson, two-year-old CJ, while waiting for the birth of their second child, our fifth grandchild. A week before Thanksgiving, a Wednesday evening, I was standing at the stove making macaroni and cheese, when my feeling became a nightmare and my life changed forever. My very pregnant daughter-in-law, LeeAnn, was washing dishes at the sink, and CJ was in his highchair eating a banana. Bill walked into the kitchen, handed me his phone, and said, "She wants to talk to you." I barely got "hello" out of my mouth before the militant-sounding woman on the phone shouted, "Give me your address now! I am sending an ambulance and the police!" Pulling the phone away from my ear, I stared at Bill and asked him, "What the heck did you say to her?" He stood there staring at me, as the woman on the phone shouted, "Are you there? Are you okay? I need your location." My strong, capable, and dependable husband of forty years stared at me, his eyes blank, his skin pale, and he had nothing to say.

Bill had been dealing with severe anxiety and depression for months. He had begun to call a counseling hotline several times a week looking for help. I have no idea what he said to the woman that night, but this time it was different, and the conversation set in motion events that would permanently change the course of our lives.

Putting the phone back to my ear, I began to try and negotiate with the woman. I told her, "I am willing to bring Bill anywhere you want. Please don't send the police or an ambulance." She told me, "No, it's not safe, give me your location immediately." My son, Jack, a pastor, had been at church leading the Wednesday night Bible study and prayer meeting. He arrived home in the middle of the conversation and walked into the kitchen, and I told the woman my son would come with me. She finally agreed that we could drive him, and she gave me an address. I knew exactly where she wanted me to take Bill. I had been there the day before with LeeAnn. It was the same hospital where she would deliver her baby at any moment. I told the woman on the phone that it would take me forty-five minutes to get to the hospital. She told me she was going to call ahead and would give me an hour. I hung up the phone, and Jack said, "Let's go, Mom." I looked at him and said, "You're not going anywhere. There is no way I am letting you leave your very pregnant wife."

I grabbed my purse, walked out to my car, and put Bill in the backseat. I buckled his seatbelt, and put the child locks on the doors. Every movement felt like it was happening in slow motion. As I slammed the car door and started the engine, I looked at Bill in the rearview mirror sitting there with a blank stare on his face. Tears were streaming down my cheeks, as I told him, "Don't move and don't speak." I then looked at my face in the mirror, in shock this was my reality. *Why is this happening? Where are you God?*

As I set off for the hospital, I turned on the radio hoping the music would calm me down. I was having a hard time concentrating, but God had a message for me as words from different worship songs began rolling around in my thoughts: *I am not alone. You, God, will give me the strength. Trust. God, You will not fail me.* I couldn't pray; I was numb, and my heart felt like it was going to explode, yet God was speaking to me through the words of these songs. By the time we arrived at the hospital, I felt calmer. I knew Bill needed help, and he was finally going to receive it.

As soon as I identified Bill to the admitting nurse, we were ushered into a long room. The room had smaller cubicles down each side and a nurse's station in the middle. It was now well after midnight, but the rooms were brightly lit and there was lots of activity. As we were shown to a cubicle, I began to realize we were not in a normal emergency room. Every wall in the unit was made of glass. They had to pull a curtain so Bill could change into a hospital gown. The curtain and gown were made of paper, and as Bill changed, I stepped out into the hall. An armed guard was standing at every door. Across the hall I could see people dressed in orange jumpsuits handcuffed to beds, and I noticed that the rooms only contained beds, with no other pieces of furniture or equipment.

I was allowed back into Bill's room, and the nurse brought in a chair for me. I pulled the chair as close to his bed as possible and sat down. The nurse wheeled in a cart, took his blood pressure, asked him some basic questions, and wheeled the cart out. We were in a room designed for his protection; even the sheets and blanket were made of paper fabric so he couldn't use them to harm himself. It became clear at the moment that he was on suicide watch. He had convinced the woman on the phone he wanted to die and had a plan to make that happen. I had brought him to a special psychiatric emergency ward to prevent him from carrying out that plan.

An hour later, a doctor wheeled in a computer and chair. I watched as he talked to Bill. "Why do you want to die? Don't you know what that will do to your family?" Chills went up my spine when the doctor's voice got parental, and he told Bill to look at me. The doctor had to verbally force Bill to look my way by saying, "I am not playing around with you. Look at her now!" Bill turned toward me and stared as the doctor said, "Do you really want to do this to her?" I watched as Bill closed his eyes and turned his head away. The truth hit me: I was not enough for my husband to want to live. I was devastated. The hurt I felt at that moment was almost more than I could handle. I had just faced a huge rejection by the one man I trusted the most—it was one of the worst moments of my life.

The doctor left the room, and the nurse motioned for me to come into the hall. I had given her my purse when we were admitted, and she handed it back to me as the doctor looked at me and said, "You can leave now, and don't come back. The guard will see you to the door. Someone will call you tomorrow when they find a bed in a secure, psychiatric facility for your husband." He then turned and walked away. The armed guard motioned for me to follow him.

"Why is this happening?" I screamed the question into the dark parking lot. I was alone, terrified, and angry. My pastor husband of forty years had been placed on a seventy-two-hour hold. I had heard jokes about being 5150'd, and I had just learned what that meant. He was now a ward of the state of California, and I had no say in the matter. As I drove home, I continued to question why this was happening. I fell asleep asking the question, dreamed it, and found the question still waiting for me when I awoke.

The next morning, sitting on the sofa at Jack's house with a cup of coffee and my Bible, I continued to ask myself and God why this was happening. I had made a commitment to watch CJ, who was still asleep, and everyone else was gone. I walked down the hall to my bedroom several times, hoping as I opened the door each time that I would find Bill sleeping in the bed. I always found the same thing though—an empty room. I was awake in the middle of a nightmare, and my life had fallen apart. It was becoming increasingly messy, and I had no idea what to do.

As I sat replaying the chaotic events from the night before in my mind, I picked up my Bible. I had been reading through the book of James during my quiet times, so I opened to that passage. I found myself staring at these words from James 1:2: "Consider it a sheer gift, friends, when tests and challenges come at you from all sides." I was facing the hardest trial of my life. My husband wanted to die—not just die; he wanted to kill himself. I was scared, feeling abandoned and alone, and I found myself struggling to wrap my head around the idea that this trial and all the chaos I was experiencing at that moment was a *gift*. I was looking in the Scriptures for comfort and direction, wanting assurance from God it was going to be all right. Instead these words felt like a cruel joke.

I decided to dig deeper and looked up that same verse in the New International Version of the Bible. I found these words jumping off the page: "Consider it pure joy." These words were worse! I was convinced there was absolutely no way I could ever consider my circumstances—the pain, fear, anger, confusion, and chaos—a gift or pure joy. I shut my Bible and slammed it down on the couch. I yelled out loud into the empty room, "I'm at my breaking point, God, and you want me to consider it a sheer gift or pure joy?"

I began to cry, which turned into sobbing, then to just plain ugly crying. I felt utterly and completely alone. Pulling a quilt up over my shoulders, I laid my head on the arm of the sofa and fell asleep. God did what He has done so many times in my life—He showed up, this time in a dream.

God took me back to a moment a few weeks earlier when I had attended a weekend retreat for ministers' wives. I had woken up at 5:00 a.m. on Saturday morning and went searching for caffeine. I located the main lodge and hot coffee. With my coffee in hand, I wandered up some stairs and found a room filled with couches. A particular sofa in a corner by the window was calling my name. As I sank into the cushions, I found myself whispering and praying, *I can't do this; I feel so helpless. Where are you, God? Why have you abandoned me?*

I closed my eyes and a movie of Elijah's story from 1 Kings 19:1–14 began playing in my mind. Elijah is afraid and running for his life. Exhausted, he finds a tree and sits down. He begins telling the Lord, "Enough of this, GOD! Take my life." An angel appears and brings food and water. The angel speaks these words, "Get up and eat! . . . You've got a long journey ahead of you." Elijah walks for forty days and forty nights, until he finally arrives at Mount Horeb. As he is lying on the floor of a cave, God shows up. He tells Elijah, "Go, stand on the mountain at attention before GOD. GOD will pass by."

As I sat watching the story play out in my mind, Elijah's face became my face. As the story continued, I became the star of the movie and I heard these words, *God is waiting for you on this mountain. Carole, God is going to reveal Himself to you this morning. Watch and listen!*

I heard a small whisper and these words:

> *Carole, you are on this mountain before Me.* I am here. I am not in the winds of a hurricane; I am not in the powerful earthquake, nor am I in the roaring of a fire. I am here with you. You will find Me in the gentle and quiet whisper of a breeze.

I felt a soft, gentle breeze pass across my face, and then I heard God say:

> Here I am. I see you. I will be with you. I know things are bad right now, and they are going to get worse. I will carry you. I am walking before you, preparing the way. You must fight and you must trust Me.

As I woke up from the dream, I felt the same gentle breeze blowing across my face. There was a fan on across the room, and it was blowing right at me. God's words were so clear, ruminating in my mind. *Here I am. I see you. I will be with you. Things are going to get worse, and I will carry you. I am walking before you, preparing the way. You must fight. You must trust me.* I knew I had a choice to make. Would I trust Him? Could I trust Him with my husband's life, the medical bills that were already more than we had in savings, and my fears of what people would say when they found out Bill wanted to kill himself?

I sat up and opened my Bible back to James. As I stared at those five verses, I realized that I had been reading them for years, and I could even recite them from memory. But every time I had read or recited them in the past, I had passed right over the message: When trials come, God is right there with me. I can trust Him in the pain. I can choose joy even when I don't understand what His plan is.

This time as I sat reading the verses, I found the comfort, encouragement, and joy that God intends us to find in the passage. These words changed the way I would look at my trials from that point forward. God had a plan. He was going to show me just how closely involved in my life He was. At that moment I had no idea where my husband was or what was happening to him, but God did. He knew exactly what was going on. James 1:5 says, "If you don't know what you're doing, pray to the Father. He loves to help." God's plans were already in motion, even though I couldn't see them. Would I fight His plans, or would I lean into them and trust Him?

I backed up and read James 1:3: "You know that under pressure, your faith-life is forced into the open and shows its true colors." I was beginning to see the first way God would use these five verses to help me respond to the mess and chaos of my life in a new way. I wasn't going to wait for understanding to trust God; I was going to grab onto Him with every ounce of determination I could muster. I cried out to God for help. I was facing a pressure like never before. My heart was heavy, tears kept falling, and my faith-life was going to be on display for everyone to see.

Over the coming months, I planted myself in these five verses. I would try to read other Scriptures, but I kept returning to these verses in James. I really needed the message I found in them, and

I read them daily and thought about them constantly. For four years, these five verses have kept me grounded and trusting God. I have learned that sometimes God needs us to concentrate on a very specific portion of Scripture because He knows it is all we can handle. This is exactly what my messy life required—a concentrated look at this portion of God's Word because that is all I could handle.

The dictionary definition of the word *joy* is, "a state of happiness or bliss."[2] Kay Warren writes, "Joy is the settled assurance that God is in control of the details of my life."[3] Psalm 16:11 (NIV) says, "You make known to me the path of life; you will fill me with joy in your presence." I have a choice in how I choose to respond to the trials, challenges, and messiness of my life. How was I going to deal with the abandonment I felt because my husband no longer wanted to be alive? My fear of finding a way to pay for the mounting medical bills? The anger and resentment I felt because I wasn't enough for him to want to live? The pressure in making decisions alone? Wait, I am not alone! God is right here. My joy comes from Him.

When Bill was released from the hospital, the depression and anxiety were still controlling his mind, but at least he had found a reason to not kill himself, a reason to live. The hardest reality for me was that when he finally found a reason to not want to kill himself, it wasn't me. It was our granddaughter; he didn't want suicide to be her memory of him. Since I had grown up with an abusive, alcoholic father who abandoned my family, my greatest hurt and fear was of being rejected. I had spent forty years loving and learning to trust Bill, and it was painful that I wasn't enough for him to want to live.

How did I deal with his rejection? To be honest, I am still working through it even after four years. I'm supposed to cling to the idea that my husband and God love me; I know this is truth, yet sometimes my disappointment causes me to question both. I have even yelled at God: *Your plan is faulty and painful. This is unfair! I have begged You over and over for answers, and You refuse to help me. I am not sure trusting You is worth it anymore.* I am sure the Enemy holds his breath with anticipation as I rage at God. How wonderful for him it would be if I turned my back on God, my faith, and my husband. I am so glad that God is patient and can handle my doubt. I recall screaming at God one afternoon. *I have had enough! I can't take it anymore!* I then heard God very clearly say, *You and Paul have something in common. Read his story and see what I mean.*

Paul asks three times that a handicap be taken away in 2 Corinthians 12:7–10. He writes, "At first I didn't think of it as a gift, and begged God to remove it. Three times I did that, and then he told me, My grace is enough, it's all you need. My strength comes into its own in your weakness. Once I heard that, I was glad to let it happen. I quit focusing on the handicap and began appreciating the gift." Like Paul, I begged God to give me answers and resolutions, but also like Paul, I needed to learn to focus on the gift of God's presence instead of the mess in my life.

Understanding came quickly. It was the same lesson I had learned in the James passage. Right now my focus was on the pain, fear, anger, and uncertainty. I begged God for answers and to take away the mess, but God wanted me to trust Him in the mess and to focus on the fact that He is in the mess with me. As I looked back over the years prior to Bill's final breakdown, I see how God had been walking before me preparing me and the way forward. Slowly I began to develop ways to cope both spiritually and emotionally.

I realized that it starts with a choice I have to make every day. How will I respond? Will I choose resentment, fear, and anger because of the mess, rejection, chaos, and uncertainty? Will I decide I can't take this or I don't deserve this? If I do, then I step onto shaky ground. This choice, and the negativity that comes with it, could lead to resentment. I might finally quit and walk away from my husband and my marriage, which would devastate my family and destroy my close relationship with God.

Or will I choose to consider all of this mess a sheer gift or pure joy? Will I keep trusting, staying committed to God and to Bill? Will I keep loving him through this illness? I must tell you it is a constant challenge. Sometimes I choose with my hands in a tight fist raised at God with anger. Other times I choose while lying face down on the floor, tears flooding my eyes. Most of the time now, however, I choose from a place of calmness, peace, and trust. But no matter which way I choose, will I choose to consider my chaotic, messy life a gift? Will I choose joy? My answer always is and always will be, yes. Daily I will choose to trust God. Daily I will choose joy. Daily I will choose!

# 3

## Facing Emotional Tumbleweeds

*When tests and challenges come at you from all sides.*
James 1:2

**Have you ever felt like you were in the middle of a movie?**
I have. One night I found myself in a scene from a movie called
*Tumbleweeds Take Over Bakersfield.* I was sitting at a fast-food
restaurant with my three oldest grandchildren, Ty, thirteen; Kinslee,
eleven; and Henry, six. It was dark outside, and out of nowhere the
wind and rain showed up. Have you ever seen it rain sideways? We
were eating, laughing, and very happy to be dry inside. A shadow
caught my eye, and the biggest tumbleweed I have ever seen rolled
right up to the window and got trapped by a fence. As we looked
out the window, we saw more coming. I have never seen so many
tumbleweeds in action at one time—they were all huge!

Our curiosity kicked in and we ventured out into the wind
and rain to check out this phenomenon. Kinslee began to free the
trapped tumbleweeds one by one. Most of them were bigger than
she was. It was funny to see this tiny girl pick up a huge tumbleweed,
toss it over the fence, and smile as the tumbleweed joined its buddies
rolling down the busy street.

I was driving to church a few days later and found myself passing pile after pile of tumbleweeds. There were hundreds of them piled up on a small stretch of road. Driving by the biggest pile, my thoughts turned dark. The pile of tumbleweeds was huge, and the tumbleweeds became ugly. Staring at the pile, tears began running down my cheeks.

I was overwhelmed again. Here I was driving to church to teach my life group, and out of the blue, a storm began to rage inside me. The tumbleweeds started coming: fear, anger, disappointment, pain, pressure, grief. I recognized them all, but this time they felt bigger. I pulled my car over to the side of the road, and I turned to God— the one person who knows it all. He has walked with me, before me, and has carried me when I couldn't go on. God's words to me that day reminded me once again that He is on this journey with me. He said, *Take a deep breath. I am here. Rest in Me, and together we will get through this. You are right where I want you to be. I am proud of how you are handling this, and I have a plan.* I wiped my tears as I realized that right in the middle of that scary, painful pile of huge, emotional tumbleweeds, there is actually a *joy* tumbleweed. I picked it up, stopped crying, and smiled.

I have discovered many ways to find my joy tumbleweed, even when there are so many other scary, painful ones. I've learned that James 1:2 doesn't say, "*If* tests and challenges come"; the verse says, "*When* tests and challenges come" (emphasis added). God tells us that tests and challenges are going to come at us from all sides. And when they do, God already knows all about them.

I have also learned that when I ask the wrong question, I have to switch and ask the right one. I was alone walking to my car on that dark, fateful morning when Section 5150 of the California Welfare Code became a part of my life. I had been kicked out of the hospital by an armed guard and told not to come back. There was nothing I could do; my husband was being transferred to a psychiatric hospital. I had no option or say in the matter. I felt helpless, I was scared, and I was mad.

I was asking the wrong question as I immediately began asking myself and God, *Why is this happening?* throughout the night and into the next morning. It took exactly thirty-seven and a half hours until I began to ask the right question. I was standing in the bathroom drying my hair, getting ready to go visit Bill at the psychiatric hospital for the first time. I stood there looking at myself in the mirror and my question changed mid-ask from, *Why is this happening?* to *Okay, this is happening, now what?* At that exact moment, my cell phone rang, and God showed up again big time. It was huge—miraculous—there was no other way to explain it other than God showed up. God had been waiting for me to ask Him the right question, and when I finally did, there He was.

The incoming call was from my son, Jack, so I picked up. The first words he said were, "I am so sorry, Mom." He went on to tell me that a pastor we knew named Deryl had called him and asked for Bill's phone number because he wanted to take Bill out for coffee. Caught off guard, Jack didn't know what to say, and the story just poured out. He told Deryl that Bill had been admitted to a psychiatric hospital because of anxiety, depression, and suicidal thoughts. Deryl asked just one question, "Where is your mom?" Jack told him I was at the house getting ready to visit Bill for the first time in the hospital. Deryl said, "By herself?"

Jack told me he thought Deryl was going to call me. I comforted Jack and told him I would be happy to talk to Deryl if he called. A few minutes later, my phone rang again. This time it was Brenda. I smiled as I answered because I knew God was up to something. You see, Brenda was a friend with whom I had reconnected and exchanged phone numbers with at the ministers' wives retreat weeks before. She is also Deryl's wife. God knew that I was going to need some love, support, and encouragement for the visit I was heading into, so He sent this couple to walk through every step with me. I answered the phone, and when I heard Brenda's voice, I burst into tears. She asked me if I could get to her house. She gave me the address, and I told her I would be there in about an hour. She told me she would accompany me to the hospital. Their sudden appearance in my life further cemented my faith in God's plan. She and her husband had personally experienced what I was going through, and they would make sure I wasn't going to go through it alone.

As I drove to Deryl and Brenda's house, I remember thinking two things. One, I needed to quit my job. And two, I needed to find someone to talk to—a therapist to help me process my circumstances. When I walked into the house, I felt warm, safe, and secure. Deryl and Brenda welcomed me and told me what I should expect during my hospital visit. I was so happy to have them guide and prepare me. As Brenda and I walked out the door, Deryl asked me if there was anything he could do for me while we were gone. I tossed out, "Yep, you can find me a therapist. I am going to need one, and you can quit my job for me." I remember his grin as he said, "I am on it." Brenda and I got into the car and drove off.

The visit was one of the scariest and most painful experiences of my life. I hardly recognized my husband when I walked into the visiting room. He was highly medicated and struggled to put sentences together. The strings from his sweatshirt hood and ties from his tennis shoes were missing. He was pale and jumpy. He told me that he was happy at the hospital and felt safe. I don't think we said more than those few words to each other, and then it was time for me to leave. As I made my way back to the lobby, I had to walk through many locked doors. As each door slammed behind me, I felt myself getting more and more emotional. I walked through the final door into the lobby, and I remember falling into Brenda's arms, sobbing. I couldn't breathe. I couldn't believe that my husband felt safe in that place and wanted to be there.

As we drove back to her house, I calmed down and began to process what I had just experienced. There were still no answers, and I was starting to realize that I had no idea what was going to happen next. I also realized that I had automatically gone to the new question: *Okay, this is happening, now what?* I was still scared, but I was no longer alone.

When Brenda and I walked back into the house that evening, Deryl greeted us with a big smile and handed me a small piece of paper. He told me he had been very busy while we were gone. Written on the paper was the name and phone number of a therapist who was expecting my call that evening. She was going to walk through the coming weeks with me and help me process everything, all at no charge. Deryl told me someone else was going to pay for my sessions. The next thing he told me was incredible. He served on the board of the organization where I currently worked. He had called the president and told him I had a family emergency. Deryl had quit my job for me, and they were going to pay me the final two months of my current contract. No questions, no explanations. God was using Deryl and Brenda to take care of us.

As I drove back to Jack's house that evening, I called my friend Nancy. I couldn't wait to fill her in on everything that had happened. Nancy had been responsible for my going to the retreat where I had reconnected with Brenda. Nancy and I have been friends for over twenty years. I still remember Nancy marching into our cabin at the retreat on Saturday afternoon, getting right in my face, and saying, "Something is terribly wrong, and you're going to tell me what it is right now." God encouraged me to tell her what was going on, so I poured out my story. She held my hand and listened as I told her I couldn't figure out what was going on. When I finished, she looked at me and asked, "How long have we been friends?" I told her more than twenty years. She then said, "You know I am a retired nurse. What I don't think you know is that I am a retired psychiatric nurse." She proceeded to show her concern for Bill and for me and also warn me that Bill was probably going to have a breakdown soon. She encouraged me to talk to my children, tell them what was going on, and let them help me. She prayed for me, cried with me, and hugged me.

As I left Deryl and Brenda's house that evening, I marveled at how God worked: He had put Nancy in my life over twenty years before because I was going to need her love, support, and knowledge about what I was going to walk through all these years later. Then He put Deryl and Brenda in my life to walk through my first visit to the psychiatric hospital, to help me quit my job, and to put me in touch with a therapist where my costs would be covered. I smiled as I picked up the phone. God was working in amazing ways to make sure I was taken care of.

God wasn't done using Deryl and Brenda in my life. We were still waiting for Jack's wife, LeeAnn, to deliver her baby, so my daughter, Kate, drove over to celebrate during the week of Thanksgiving. Tuesday morning before Thanksgiving, I was looking through a phone book trying to find a hotel I could afford. Bill was going to be released the next day and would be starting a comprehensive, four-week, outpatient program in San Bernardino the following week. Deryl had been calling me every day to check on me, so when I saw his name on my phone, I picked up. He asked me what I was doing, and I filled him in on my search for a hotel. He asked about the program times and location. I told him the address and that Bill had to be in a four-hour therapy session Monday through Friday for four weeks. I can still hear his laugh as he said, "I have the answer. We live very close to that location. Brenda and I have an extra master suite over our garage. The room is yours for the next four weeks. When do you want to move in?" I couldn't believe they were opening their home to us. Through my tears, I said, "Friday." Bill was released from the psychiatric hospital the night before Thanksgiving. I was thankful to have my family together.

On Friday morning, we moved into Deryl and Brenda's home. For the next four weeks, I felt wrapped in a warm cocoon of care and love. Every morning, I would wake up to coffee and a fire. Every evening after dinner, Brenda and I would sit by the fire and watch a movie. I spent my mornings reading in my car in the parking lot waiting for Bill to finish his therapy sessions and my afternoons curled up with a cup of tea, reading by the fire.

I had learned that trials will come, and I had to ask the right question. I was now learning the next lesson: when God sends people, let them in. I could have ignored God and not told Nancy what was going on, but I was faithful in my vulnerability. That willingness to be vulnerable, transparent, and raw with her opened the door so Nancy could love me, encourage me, guide me, and pray for me. I could have refused to answer the phone when Brenda called, but I was brave. I could have told Deryl that I was okay and didn't need anything, but I was honest. I was so embarrassed by my need of somewhere to live that I could have said no to Deryl when he offered us a room, but I humbly accepted. My bravery, honesty, and humility opened the door so Deryl and Brenda could meet my immediate needs. I was confused, scared, and lost. Deryl, Brenda, and Nancy provided space for me to talk or not, cry, sleep, and begin to heal.

The second I stared in the mirror at thirty-seven and a half hours and said to God, *Okay, this is happening, now what?* was the moment I saw God in action and realized how much He loved and cared for me. God was already there working and taking care of me, just as He had promised. I asked God, *Now what?* and He sent Nancy, Deryl, and Brenda, and I let them in. I am also glad they listened when God told them to help me, and they willingly reached out. God uses people like you and me to help people like you and me.

Why was it so important for me to change my question that day? Would God have still shown up? Yes. God would have still shown up, but I might have missed it. When I kept asking God, *Why is this happening?* I was focused on the pain and the problem—the pile of tumbleweeds that seemed too overwhelming and too big. When my question changed to, *Okay, this is happening, now what?* I became calm, and I was now open to a world of possibilities. My eyes were no longer focused on the big pile anymore; I was now focused on the joy tumbleweed that told me I wasn't alone. I remember telling God, as I stared in the mirror the morning after taking Bill to the psychiatric emergency room, that I trusted Him. I knew that He would show me what to say and do.

God tells us that tests and challenges will come at us from all sides. He also tells us that He has a plan and that He promises to be there. Oftentimes He sends people to help. Psalm 5:11 says, "But you'll welcome us with open arms when we run for cover to you." Asking Him the right question means I will trust Him and lean into the pain, learning whatever it is He needs me to learn. My God welcomes me with open arms, so I run to Him for cover.

As I type this, I pray that there is someone reading these words who needs to hear this message, these verses, and my words. You are not alone. God sees you! Do you feel windblown? Are the tumbleweeds, the trials, coming at you from all sides? Let's dig through the pile of tumbleweeds coming at us together and find that one tumbleweed marked *joy*. The biggest need I had that day was to know I was not alone. Hear me say: you are not alone. God sees us and knows where we are. Let's run to Him for cover. He will show up big time, and I promise, His arms are big enough for all of us.

# 4

## The Source of My Strength, Power, and Joy

*Ask boldly, believingly, without a second thought.*
James 1:5

The first Christmas after Bill came home from the psychiatric hospital was also our first Christmas in our new home in Bakersfield. We came home from Deryl and Brenda's house a week before Christmas, and I decided that year not to decorate. I just wasn't in the mood. Christmas decorating had lost its fun when we moved to Fairfield. Every Christmas since I have struggled with the memory of the day, I stood by the dumpster in the church parking lot in tears. My morning started out so exciting—we were finally moving into our new home in Fairfield, after six months in a hotel room. We had borrowed a trailer and were moving our possessions from storage. The six-foot-by-six-foot storage unit contained my prized Christmas decorations and my beloved washer and dryer. They had been in storage for more than two years now, and I couldn't wait to see them. I was surprised when our first stop with the loaded trailer was the church parking lot. My tears were because Bill had discovered a nasty problem with our stuff.

As we pulled into the parking lot of the church in Fairfield, Bill looked at me and said, "I need to tell you something. I noticed when we moved our stuff here six months ago that we might have had a rat problem." While we lived in Newhall, we had stored our stuff in a friend's garage for the two years. He lived out in the country, and rats had set up house in my boxes of Christmas decorations and my beloved washer and dryer. Bill had noticed it when we moved our stuff to the storage unit in Fairfield but decided to wait to tell me. We had sold everything when we moved from Fresno to Newhall, and these were the only possessions I had left; he knew it would be devastating for me. From the moment we had signed the papers, I had been imagining the appliances in my new laundry room and where each of my Christmas decorations would go. Why was Bill just now telling me we might have a rat problem?

One by one the boxes came off the trailer. We opened them and found remnants of a rat hotel. It smelled so bad, and I had to turn away from the mess in each box. It was a horror story: *Rats Destroy Christmas for Carole*. As each box was opened and we found nothing could be salvaged, I became more and more emotional. I completely lost it when Bill opened the box with my most prized Christmas decoration—a nativity set made of olive tree wood that we had purchased on a trip to Israel. It was the first decoration I put out each year and the last one to be packed up. I already had a special place picked out in my new home for it—an alcove in the wall where it was the first thing you would see when you walked in my front door. I had planned to put it out that day. I stood there in tears, holding my breath as Bill tried to unwrap, with gloves on, each piece of the set. Piece by piece was completely destroyed, chewed on, and the rats had used this particular box as a birthing room, bathroom, or maybe both. When he unwrapped the manger with baby Jesus lying in it, I almost threw up. The rats had chewed the head off baby Jesus.

As I stared at the headless baby in the manger, tears flowing, I actually struggled to throw it in the dumpster. Looking back now,

I realize that I somehow knew my world was on shaky ground. Something was not right with Bill, and each day he was becoming more and more unstable. I heard God say to me that day as I tossed the headless figure into the dumpster, *Carole, don't trust in the stuff, trust in Me. I am the source of your strength, power, and joy. I will take care of you.*

We drove with the almost empty trailer to our new home. My treasured washer and dryer were put in the garage until a man from our church could come over and help Bill investigate the damage to them. I was not allowed in the garage to see the mess on the day they cleaned them out. Bill knew if I saw the mess, I would never use them again. Bill and the man spent hours with a hose and cleaning solutions trying to salvage the appliances. When they finally got them usable and put them in place in my new laundry room, it took me four weeks to put the first load of clothes in, and I washed that load six times. I never put a load in them again without thinking of the rats. When we sold the house, the new owners made them a part of the deal, and I was happy to say goodbye to them.

We had arrived in Bakersfield late the night before. I still had a few days and was trying to motivate myself to decorate. I have always loved Christmas and decorating. I might have been known to even go a little bit overboard. Would this be the year? Nope, the rats changed all that. Christmas decorating doesn't hold the same excitement for me. Early Sunday morning a week before Christmas, I sat with my coffee listening to Bill snore in the bedroom. I was thanking God that he was alive and trying to find hope. I picked up my Bible and it opened to Nehemiah. I knew his story; Nehemiah was a man who cared. He left the comfort of a palace, where he was as close to the king as you could get. He was the cupbearer, the man who tasted any food or drink before the king to protect him from being poisoned. He left it all to return home to Jerusalem to help the people rebuild the wall. He encouraged the people through the danger and opposition they faced in completing the project. He led the people to finish rebuilding the wall in fifty-two days.

As I sat that morning skimming through his story, I read Nehemiah 8:10, and God spoke to me through the words I read. "This day is holy to God. Don't feel bad. The joy of GOD is your strength." As I sat looking at my undecorated house, I began to feel sorry for myself. It was Sunday, and I felt bad and alone. My daughter and her family were sleeping in the rooms upstairs. They would wake up and begin getting ready for church any minute. I wanted normal. I wanted security. But all I had was insecurity and fear. I asked God to show me what to do. I reread the words from Nehemiah 8:10 and God spoke. He said, *Get up, get dressed, go to church. I am here and today is a day to find joy in Me. Wait and see. I am the source of your strength and joy.*

James 1:5 says, "Ask boldly, believingly, without a second thought." I boldly asked God to show me what to do. He clearly showed me that morning, so I got up and went to church. As I listened to the sermon, I knew that I needed to join the church. During the invitation, God said, *You want normal? Join the church this morning.* I turned to Bill and said, "You can sit here, but I need normal, so I am joining the church right now. Come with me or stay, but I am going." He was really struggling that morning with his anxiety and depression. He didn't want to be left in the pew alone, so we walked the aisle and joined Valley Baptist Church. I was starting to find normal, but God was not done that day. He was going to show me security and how much He loved me.

There are times when my bold ask of God, *Show me what to do*, gets a bit sarcastic, and I find myself saying, *Okay, how are You going to fix this one?* I remember saying those exact words to God in my car after church, right after purchasing $140 worth of steaks. It was the week before Christmas, and I had promised months before to bring the steaks to our family Christmas Day dinner the next weekend. I was asked to purchase them from a particular butcher, and I had agreed. When I made this promise, life was normal. Bill and I were both working, and we had enough money to cover the expense.

Now I had no job, we lived on Bill's retirement and social security, and I was struggling to find a way to pay the mounting medical bills as well as our daily living expenses. I had to give the psychiatric hospital my credit card the month before so they could charge over $6,000 to get Bill released, because our insurance wouldn't cover it. I had just gotten a bill from the ambulance company that week for over $2,000 for taking Bill from the psychiatric emergency room to the hospital—again my insurance wouldn't cover it. So I was facing an $8,000 credit card bill when I said to God, *How are You going to fix this one?* I was talking about the steaks at that moment, and hadn't even begun to talk to Him about the credit card debt.

As I sat in the car that afternoon with the very expensive meat in a bag on my lap, I had no idea how I was going to pay for those steaks. At this point, you may be wondering why I still chose to purchase the steaks or why I didn't just buy cheaper ones. Well we had just come home from San Bernardino, and it was our first Christmas since Bill had been released from the psychiatric hospital. He was still struggling, and I needed normal. I wanted to honor my commitment and do exactly what I said I would do, so I bought the steaks.

As I was driving home from the butcher shop, I told God again, much nicer this time, to show me how to pay for these steaks. As the verse in James 1:5 says, I asked God boldly, and I expected Him to show up. My initial thought was that our family knew our circumstances, and someone would offer to help pay for the steaks. Everyone knew how expensive they would be.

I got home and handed the steaks off to my son-in-law, Luke. He was beyond excited to see the sticker on the package and that I had gotten them from his favorite butcher. His excitement was contagious, and I decided that I was going to relax and trust God, so I could enjoy the dinner the next weekend. I knew those steaks would be delicious, and I knew God was going to show me how to pay for them.

I walked into my apartment, dropped the car keys on my desk, and saw the pile of mail from the day before. I felt God say, *Look in the pile.* As I moved the envelopes around, I feared another bill when an envelope caught my eye. It was from my bank and looked like a check. I was curious and opened it. Inside was a letter and a check. The letter said, "In reviewing our records, we discovered that when you refinanced your home on Prescott Lane in 2014, we made an error in the fees that we charged you. Attached is a check for $81.07 to reimburse you for the mistake." I smiled because I knew we had two rental properties and had refinanced both of them at that same time. I looked through the mail and found a second envelope from my bank, and inside was the same letter, this time for our rental on Todd Heddrick Lane, with a check for $59.10. The two checks equaled $140.17, enough to pay for the steaks I had just purchased, with seventeen cents left over. God had been planning this solution for two years.

God wasn't done. Over the past year, my sister-in-law, Sandy, had become a source of encouragement and strength for me. When Bill had gone into the hospital, she was in constant communication with me, checking on me to make sure I was doing okay and always asking if I needed anything. She knew my love for Christmas decorations, and she knew about the rats destroying my decorations. She had been with me in Israel when I purchased my nativity set. We had laughed when I finally was able to tell her about the rats eating baby Jesus, and we hoped they had gotten really sick. I got a package from her a few days later in the mail with a note that said, "I forgot I had this. When I found it, I wanted you to have it."

When I opened the package, it was pieces of a similar nativity set like the one the rats had eaten. She had bought one in the same shop in Israel on our trip. This set was bigger, with more pieces, and I just had to build it. I smiled as I thought back to the story I read in Nehemiah the past Sunday about how he helped to build the wall. I remember standing in front of the dumpster in Fairfield, as I was tossing the headless baby Jesus in, when God said, *Carole, don't trust in the stuff, trust in Me. I am the source of your strength, power, and joy. I will take care of you.* God had provided a way to pay for the steaks and now was giving me a bigger nativity set to build and enjoy. God truly is the source of my strength, power, and joy.

If you were to open my favorite Bible to Psalm 119:97–120, you would find the three words *clarity*, *hope*, and *joy* written at the bottom of the page. I love verse 105 (NIV), "Your word is a lamp for my feet, a light on my path." I read this verse and thanked God at that moment for providing the money for the steaks, for the beautiful nativity set, and for showing me what to do. I have now added the words *power* and *strength* to the bottom of that page.

But what happens when I ask boldly for God to show up, and He takes so long? I start second guessing. It has been five years, and my husband is still struggling with depression and anxiety; the fears are still there, and we have no answers. I stare at those five words—clarity, hope, strength, power, and joy—and ask and plead with God:

> *Where are You, God? Where is the clarity? Where is the hope?* I desperately need Your strength and power. How do You expect me to have joy? When I find myself at a place in life when hope is elusive and when You are silent—with no check, no answer, no response, no clarity—what do I do then? What do I do when I feel weak and powerless and when finding joy can be a struggle?

I read another one of my favorite Bible stories, Matthew 14:22–34. I love Peter and can relate to him in so many ways. This story in Matthew is my favorite Peter story. Jesus has just performed His most public miracle, feeding over five thousand people with five loaves of bread and two fish. He then sent the disciples out onto the sea in a boat, and He stayed behind to spend time alone and to pray. While the boat was far from the shore, the winds came and began to rock the boat. The men were terrified as they saw a figure walking toward them on the water. Jesus told them it's Him, and not to be afraid. Here is my favorite part of the story:

> Peter suddenly bold, said, "Master, if it's really you, call me to come to you on the water."
>
> Jesus said, "Come ahead."
>
> Jumping out of the boat, Peter walked on the water to Jesus. But when he looked down at the waves churning beneath his feet, he lost his nerve and started to sink. He cried, "Master, save me!"
>
> Jesus didn't hesitate. He reached down and grabbed his hand. Then he said, "Faint-heart, what got into you?"
>
> The two of them climbed into the boat and the wind died down. (Matthew 14:28–32)

The truth I needed to hear jumped off the page. The disciples had just seen a miracle in the feeding of all those people, a moment only explained by God's actions. Yet only a few hours later, they were terrified, scared, and alone as the waves pounded their tiny boat. Peter questioned Jesus by saying, "If it's really you, call for me to come to you on the water." As long as his focus was on Jesus, he walked on the waves with no problem. The minute his focus went to the waves beneath his feet, he started to sink.

This is so me. I find myself doing this exact same thing. God shows up and provides money for steaks and a bigger and better nativity set, but I remain focused on needing the answers to my big questions. How am I going to be able to pay the $8,000 credit card bill the next week? What is going to happen to Bill, and what do I do next? When I take my eyes off Jesus and, like Peter, fix my sight on what's frightening me, I become "faint-hearted."

When I ask questions of God with my attention fixed on my circumstances, it causes anger, fear, resentment, and confusion. I begin yelling at God and demanding answers. I have to make a choice. Will I continue on this path, or will I fix my attention back on God and give Him my fears, burdens, and pain? Will I trust that He has a plan even when He is taking too long, from my perspective, and not giving me my answers? Will I continue to ask boldly, believing without a second thought and expecting Him to show up?

The answer is yes! While I demand answers and tell God what I need, He demands my total surrender to trust Him completely. Sometimes He answers immediately, like the checks for the steaks at the exact moment I needed it. Other times I have to wait for the answers, like wondering how I am going to pay the credit card bill or my questions about Bill. And I have to accept that I may never get some answers until I am sitting on God's lap in heaven, such as finding out why this happened to Bill.

Joy is not dependent on circumstances. It comes from building a foundation on Jesus by studying God's Word and trusting Him with my circumstances. God says we can have joy no matter what is going on in our lives, and I believe Him.

How can we be prepared for those times when life gets messy, and hope, power, strength, and joy are nowhere to be found? When rats eat baby Jesus, when the credit card bill is huge and coming due, and when we have promised to buy steaks we can't afford? We stop being "faint-hearted" and choose to fix our attention on God, read His Word, and trust Him. Psalm 119:114 (NIV) says, "You are my refuge and my shield; I have put my hope in your word." He is our place of safety, our protector, and we must run to Him. We are to choose to fix our attention on God, not on the waves below our feet, and to put our hope in Him, trusting that things will work out. And with this choice, that's when hope, strength, power, and joy return.

Right about now, you are reading this and saying, "She forgot clarity." I didn't. I find my clarity from this statement, and you can too. I have this truth written on several sticky notes and placed in locations where I can read them regularly, "I belong to the God of the Bible. He knows my circumstances, and He's got this. This is clarity enough for me."

# 5

## The Difference between Living in Fear and Living with It

*So don't try to get out of anything prematurely.*
James 1:3

*What if?* became the question I tormented myself with for two years after Bill was released from the psychiatric hospital. I would play the what-if game about the past. What if I had seen this coming? What if I did something to cause his breakdown? What if I could have prevented this? Then I would switch to the future: What if I can't help him? What if the suicidal thoughts come back? What if we can't find medication that works, or what if the medication stops working? What will happen if he stops the medication again?

To complicate things, I felt an intense amount of pressure from Bill's needs. He said to me over and over, "I need your help. You will help me, won't you? Promise me, you will help me." My spirit almost broke when Bill's psychiatrist and case worker both started telling me the same thing every time I spoke to them. They both told me repeatedly, "Just keep him alive until we figure this out. Just keep him alive until we find the right medication. Just keep him alive."

Between my what-if questions and being told to *just keep him alive*, the pressure began to take a toll on my own health.

I had been seeing a counselor, and at the end of our third session, he bluntly said, "I'm sorry; I can't help you. Your husband is suffering with mental illness, and he needs help. I don't know what to say to you that will help you through this. I got nothing, and I don't want to keep taking your money." It was raining as I walked out of the counselor's office that afternoon. I sat in my car, crying, frustrated, angry, and worn out. I closed my eyes and began to listen to the rain on the roof of the car, turning to the One who had repeatedly shown up over and over.

I began to talk to God, *He's got nothing? How can a trained counselor not know what to say that can help me?* As I sat there crying and praying, I heard God speak to me very clearly. *Carole, you have to let Bill go. It is not your job to keep him alive. You can't change, stop, or fix this. Bill is in My hands; you can't keep him from killing himself; you can't keep him alive—that is My job. Let him go! Your job is to love him and trust Me.*

Wow! Letting go seemed like the most irresponsible thing to do, yet that is what He said to do. I am a get-it-done gal, and I protect those who belong to me, like a mama pit bull. Now God was telling me to not only let go, but that Bill belongs to Him and not to me.

With the rain pelting the roof of my car, it felt like this truth was being driven into my brain. I sat for a long time listening to the rain. My tears dried up, and I took a deep breath. I whispered, *Okay, God. I will give him to You.* I cupped my hands in front of my face and imagined placing Bill in my hands. Then I lifted my hands up, and out loud, said to God, *Here he is.* I then turned my hands over and put them back in my lap. The weight I had felt, the pressure, all of it was gone. I felt free for the first time in a long while. I have had to repeat this action many times over the last four years when I realize that I am again feeling pressured and taking on responsibility for Bill.

That day in the car I realized that even though I had released my responsibility for Bill to God, I still had to live with the real fear of Bill's illness. There was a real possibility that he might not get better or that he may even get worse and kill himself. Trusting God by giving Bill to God didn't take away my fear, but I had begun to learn the lesson of living *with* fear, not living *in* fear.

Living *in* fear is taking charge in an unhealthy way. When I live in fear, I am either trying to relive the past or pre-live the future. This is where my what-if questions originate from. *What if I had only . . . ?* is a question of trying to change the past. I can't go back to past experiences; they have already happened and are now a permanent part of my life. When my what-if questions become, *What if this happens . . . ?* I start taking charge of things that have not happened or may never happen. I begin to imagine circumstances and preplan my reactions. When I am caught up and living in fear, I am trying to control circumstances that are out of my control, both past and future ones. This drains my energy, and I become angry and afraid all over again.

Living *with* fear means I am living in the moment; I stop asking, *What if?* and start asking, *What now?* God shows up every time when I live in the moment and ask Him, *What now?*

Remember the $8,000 credit card bill for the hospital and ambulance? I was living in fear, totally consumed, when it was time to pay the credit card bill. I barely had enough money in our bank account to pay the minimum payment. We had never in our marriage carried a balance on a credit card, and I was faced with being the one to make it happen. Remember the check that came from the bank that helped pay for the steaks? As I sat praying about what to do with the credit card, I remembered that we still owned those two rental properties that we had refinanced and that God had used to pay for the steaks.

The first rental property had been our main home when we lived in Fresno. We had used a credit line on the equity from that house to help purchase a home for our daughter, Kate, and her husband, Luke. Luke also worked for the foundation in Fresno. We couldn't afford to sell either home when both Luke and Bill lost their jobs. We refused to walk away and turn the properties over to the bank, so we found a property manager and turned both homes into rentals. We had been renting them for five years, waiting for the market to change, so we could sell them without taking a huge financial loss.

I looked up the information for the line of credit on my bank website and discovered that we had an available balance I could transfer immediately into my checking account. In other words, I had access to the amount of money I needed to pay the credit card bill, and the monthly payment would only go up ten dollars a month on the loan. It would have been easy to bolt on those houses and just walk away five years ago when Bill lost his job. We could have tried to get out of the mortgages prematurely by turning both homes back over to the bank, but instead we had chosen to honor our commitment in purchasing them and found a way to make it work for all those years. The blessing was that in our commitment to hang on to the houses, they were now providing a low-interest way for me to pay the medical bills. God provided the way once again. We can live *with* fear and not *in* fear, because we live *with* a faithful God.

When you love someone who struggles with anxiety, depression, and suicidal thoughts, it can be easy to fall into living in fear. Bill's mental illness means he struggles daily with anger, paranoia, mood swings, withdrawal, and negativity. One of the side effects of Bill's anxiety and depression is a need for control. When he feels like he is out of control, he thinks I must be the cause of his discomfort, and he gets angry and starts yelling at me and blaming me for everything wrong in his world. I know when this happens that he is just saying anything to take away the pressure and the pain, but he has said some pretty crazy and painful things to me in his out-of-control anger.

I have to choose daily how to handle these circumstances and find joy when Bill's struggles are turned on me. Dealing with my fear has taught me that God designed fear with two purposes—it can be a protector or a motivator. Using this knowledge, I have taken these purposes and developed some practical coping skills that help me survive when Bill struggles, especially when he starts blaming me for his problems.

**When I use fear as a protector . . .**

*I create a safe zone.* I was standing in my garage one afternoon throwing a fit, yelling at God, shouting, *Enough is enough! I need answers! There has to be a reason for Bill's depression and anxiety.* I was telling God that it had been going on too long, that I was exhausted, and that He either needed to fix it or tell me what was going on. I stomped my foot while I was not-so-quietly filling God in. Hearing my foot hit the concrete floor, I knew I was caught in the battle of living in fear and control again. I took a deep breath and asked God to please forgive me.

I stood there, calming down, thinking I needed to create a visual to help get me back to living with fear, so I would stop living in fear and trying to control everything—a way I could visually give it all to God. I saw a tape measure and duct tape on the tool bench and picked them up. I measured out and taped off a three-foot square on the floor of my garage. I told God that by stepping into the square, I was giving Him everything. I would trust Him for everything inside the square and everything outside the square. I was going to live with fear, trusting Him in the moment and letting Him deal with the future. He could handle it all. I took a deep breath and stepped into the square. The square became a safe zone. The act of stepping into the square took all the pressure out of my system, and I felt so much calmer. This became my visual for releasing my stresses to God whenever the pressure starts backing up. I look down and imagine I am recreating that three-foot square. I draw imaginary lines on the ground in front of me, then I step into the square as an act of giving it all to God.

This can be a helpful tool when any kind of fear overtakes you. Start talking to God, and imagine drawing a three-foot-by-three-foot square on the ground in front of you. Tell God you are going to let Him handle it all, inside the square and outside the square. Once you have imagined drawing the square, it is very important that you actually step into it. The act of stepping into the square is similar to me lifting my cupped hands with Bill in them and turning him over to God. These acts are symbolic of choosing to live in the moment. The square reminds me I am not in charge. I have created imaginary squares in many places; once I even stood and created one on an airplane.

*I listen to my "When Life Gets Scary" playlist.* I created a playlist I call, "When Life Gets Scary." I turn it on when the pressure or fear starts to get to me. God has given me three worship songs in particular that are on this list that give me peace: "Even If," by MercyMe; "Oh My Soul," by Casting Crowns; and "While I Wait," by Lincoln Brewster. I can't count how many times this scenario has played out in the past years: Bill starts yelling, so I turn on my playlist, hit shuffle, and start praying. When the music is playing softly in the background of our home or car and one of these three songs starts to play, the words and music soothe me and remind me that this is all a temporary trial that I will get through.

*I live with my palms facing up.* Other times when Bill starts yelling, I start praying, I ask God to tell me what to say, or more importantly, what not to say. Just when I'm about to say something that will make things worse, an interruption happens, and I hear God say, *This is your chance; change what you were going to say or say nothing.* When Bill starts yelling he can't control himself; it is a part of his illness, but it still hurts. I began to wonder though if perhaps there was a way for him to vent but have his words not affect me? I began praying for a way to live with, but not absorb, the hurtful words he says when he yells.

One day Bill was yelling and I was praying, God told me, *Look at your hands.* I looked down at my hands and they were tightly gripping my thighs. I had been finding bruises on my thighs for months and wondering where they were coming from. Now I had my answer; I was leaving the bruises myself. I could feel the tension all the way up to the top of my head. As soon as I realized what I was doing, I let go of my thighs and turned my palms over and laid them back down in my lap. The tension left immediately. I sat there with my palms facing up as Bill was still yelling. I started to imagine the hurtful, painful words going into my ears, down my arms, and big, angry speech bubbles floating up into the air from my open palms. I had stopped listening to words I didn't need to hear anyway. I found it. This was a way to allow Bill to vent without me absorbing it.

As I watched the flow of his words go in my ear and down my arm, I realized that the words bypassed my brain, so I never remembered them and they missed my heart, not leaving a lasting hurt. My focus instead became holding my palms facing up on my thighs. Try it; it is not a natural behavior, and it is a great distraction when you are in a circumstance where you must listen but not hear or absorb what is being said.

**When I use fear as a motivator . . .**

*I live in care, not control.* Nights are particularly hard because Bill struggles when he sleeps. He has really bad nightmares and thrashes around. Most nights his body twitches from the pressure his anxiety puts in his system. Sometimes I lay in bed in the dark and pray he will find some relief. After five years of this, my morning usually starts out with the same ritual. I take a few deep breaths and stretch, then I spend a few moments looking inside at my emotions. I look inside for the dialogue that is starting and the thoughts racing through my mind. If my initial thoughts are fearful, my inner dialogue sounds like this: *I can't handle this. I didn't sign up for this. When is this going to stop? I don't deserve this. I am going to call the doctor and make him increase his medica*tion. *I know there has to be an answer, and I am going to find it.* These types of thoughts that are focused on myself tell me I am living in fear and trying to take control.

If my morning thoughts start with a prayer, it keeps the focus off myself: *God, help Bill rest for the next few hours. I will bake his favorite cookies. Today let's go to his favorite restaurant. I think there is a new episode of his favorite show out. How can I make today special?* This care dialogue sounds much different from the control one. Care is realizing I can't stop, fix, or change the circumstances.

I don't ask Bill how he is feeling when he gets out of bed. I give him time to tell me if he wants to. Care is finding ways to be loving and helpful. Control is what I interpret James warning about in James 1:3, "Don't try to get out of anything prematurely." Control causes me to be negative, to try to find any way out of the circumstances, to bolt before the blessing. Care motivates me to speak kindly, to be positive, to keep loving and caring for Bill, and to know God has a plan and He is the one in control.

*I love my husband three seconds at a time.* One afternoon I was talking to my friend and therapist, Greg. Most of our sessions come at a point of crisis when I am either physically tired, emotionally exhausted, or just plain mad. What I call a *survival session* is when all three hit me at once. One day during a survival session, Greg told me I needed to start living in the moment. I was telling him that I could sense when Bill's controlling anger was coming. I knew from experience how painful these episodes were, and I felt totally helpless. It felt like I was watching a huge wave out in the distance as it was getting bigger and bigger and coming to knock me over. As we talked, I realized that I had a tendency to start reacting before the wave even got to me. Greg told me that I had to stop looking out on the horizon at the coming wave and instead bring myself back into the moment. I needed to ride the current wave instead of focusing on the huge one coming. I couldn't stop the coming wave anyway, and I had no idea if or how long it would take to get to me. I told Greg that I had been reading a book that talked about building relationships and loving someone thirty seconds at a time.

I told him, "Thirty seconds is too long when the crisis hits, so I am going to start loving Bill three seconds at a time."

After our session I continued to think about this idea of loving three seconds at a time. The next time Bill started in with the anger and yelling, I immediately started counting in my mind, one and breathe . . . two and breathe . . . three and breathe . . . then I repeated the process. Success; it worked! I could manage three seconds. I could love Bill three seconds at a time. Using the three-seconds-at-a-time process will help you with living and loving in the current moment. Try it—it works. I also hope you will discover, like I did, that by anticipating the wave you see coming and starting to react to it, the situation becomes bigger than it might otherwise have been by just staying focused on the current wave of the moment.

Here is the question that helps me determine whether I am living with fear or in fear: *Where are you, God?* When this question begins rolling around in my mind, I know my focus has moved from God to my circumstances. When I become aware of this question and where my focus is, I take action to immediately stop whatever I am doing to change my focus. If I am in bed, I get up; if I am out running errands, I go sit in my car; if I can't get somewhere alone, I close my eyes and shut out everything around me. I must change my focus or my what-if questions return. I have a note stuck to the window of my office with this psalm written on it. I also have it written on a note in my phone and in my Bible so I have access to it wherever I am and can receive the encouragement it provides me. I get alone with God and read these words out loud, if possible, imagining the "I" is me talking to God.

Be good to me, God—and now!
I've run to you for dear life.
I'm hiding out under your wings
until the hurricane blows over.
I call out to High God,
the God who holds me together.

He sends orders from heaven and saves me,
he humiliates those who kick me around.
God delivers generous love,
he makes good on his word.
I find myself in a pride of lions
who are wild for a taste of human flesh;
Their teeth are lances and arrows,
their tongues are sharp daggers.
Soar high in the skies, O God!
Cover the whole earth with your glory!
They booby-trapped my path;
I thought I was dead and done for.
They dug a mantrap to catch me,
and fell in headlong themselves.
I'm ready, God, so ready,
ready from head to toe,
Ready to sing, ready to raise a tune:
"Wake up, soul!
Wake up, harp! Wake up, lute!
Wake up, you sleepyhead sun!"
I'm thanking you, God, out loud in the streets,
singing your praises in town and country.
The deeper your love, the higher it goes;
every cloud is a flag to your faithfulness.
Soar high in the skies, O God!
Cover the whole earth with your glory! (Psalm 57:1–11)

David wrote this psalm while hiding in a cave from King Saul, who was trying to kill him. He ran to God for protection. As I read David's words, or speak them out loud, they become my own personal cry to God. When I read verse 1, I see that David's focus is not on the army, the men chasing him, the possibility that he could be killed, or even the cave where he is hiding. He is not crying out, *Where are you, God?* He knows God is right there. His words, "I've run to you for dear life," tell me that living with fear is possible only when I run to God for dear life, like David did.

As I read the final verses of David's cry, his words turn to praise, and I am challenged to turn my fear into praise too. I open up the music app on my phone to my "When Life Gets Scary" playlist, and I find a particular song. As Lincoln Brewster's song, "Worship While I Wait," begins to play, I am now living with fear, not in it. I am now like David crying out to the One who holds me together, and I am so ready, from head to toe, to sing His praises, while I live with fear and wait.

# Facing the Opposition That Comes with Obedience

*You know that under pressure, your faith-life is forced into the open and shows its true colors.*

James 1:3

"It's not contagious!" I have wanted to scream those words at so many people over the past four years. The first time was in October 2017. I was attending a convention for California Southern Baptist churches, and I had a job to set up a booth for one of the denominational organizations. Bill was helping me set up the night before the convention began, and there were a few other people in the building also setting up booths. I looked up just as two men we knew walked into the room. I saw them stop in the doorway when they saw us, say something to each other, look our way again, and then turn around and walk back out the door. These were two men who would have approached us before my husband began to struggle with depression, anxiety, and suicidal thoughts. They would have walked right over and talked to us before. We had considered them friends.

My heart broke into a million pieces at that point. All I wanted to do was finish and get out of the building quickly. No one spoke to us that night—no one. We finished our task and returned to our hotel. As I lay in bed trying to sleep, I prayerfully decided that I was going to ask Bill not to return to the convention with me the next day. I didn't have to ask; he woke up the next morning in a full-blown panic attack and decided to stay in the hotel.

I attended some of the meetings and fulfilled my job responsibilities. As I ran into person after person I knew, I felt completely disconnected. Somehow it seemed that Bill's struggles had changed me. It felt like people avoided eye contact so they didn't have to speak to me. I felt like a stranger to people I had known for years. Only one person asked me that day how Bill was doing, and then he quickly stopped the conversation, saying, "I forgot I am late. I have to be somewhere." It seemed as if he wanted to be anywhere but talking to me at that moment.

I remember trying to talk to someone at the convention who I knew was in leadership. I tried to explain the isolation and the disconnection I was feeling. I told him I knew I was not alone; I was aware of other pastors and their families in similar circumstances. I was struggling to find any resources to help us. His response was to stare at me and say, "What in the world do you think we can do to help?" As he walked away, the reality set in—I didn't fit in anymore, and there was no help to be found here. I felt contagious. I began to struggle with understanding that no one wants to or knows how to deal with the problems mental health issues bring, especially when a pastor struggles with mental illness. I felt that Bill and I were a spectacle. I wondered, *Is everyone staring at me?*

I came home from the convention that year with a huge amount of guilt. I blamed myself, as I had promised God before any of this had happened that I would be transparent and nothing in my life would be off-limits. I had been a speaker and teacher for women's retreats and conferences for more than twenty years. I had loved traveling all over the country and sharing stories about my life and about how God healed my rejection and identity issues that resulted from being raised by an abusive father. I told God I wanted the experiences of my life to be used for His glory and had launched a website called Carole's Journey, sharing authentically about my life. I had no idea, however, just how transparent He would ask me to be.

When Bill came home from the hospital and completed his four weeks of intense, outpatient therapy, we returned home to Bakersfield, and it felt natural that God would ask me to blog about the experience. God told me to share what He was doing in our lives with anyone who would listen or read about it. I kept telling God, *We don't have a solution yet, so I can't tell them the end of the story*. But God said He wanted people to watch the story unfold. I was obedient and wrote the blog and posted it in January, two months after his initial crisis. I shared in detail about Bill's battle with anxiety, depression, and suicidal thoughts. I wanted others to understand the deep struggles of our journey, and I was transparent about the fears, tears, anger, and uncertainty. I also shared about the ways God had already shown up. Over five thousand people read the blog post over the first two weeks.

A few days following the blog post, I received an email from a pastor who told me to grab a cup of coffee and read a blog that he thought would help me. The blog started out by describing how hard it was being Job's wife. The blogger spoke about being a broken-down, miserable, life-weary woman who finally turns back to God. I remember sitting and reading, then rereading the blog, asking myself if this is really what I was. I called my friend Elizabeth, who knows me well. I forwarded the blog to her and asked her, "Is this me?" She called me immediately; her first words were, "No, it is not!" She said that either this pastor didn't know me at all or hadn't read my blog to the end.

A few days later, another email came, asking me why I was airing my dirty laundry for all the world to read? I was dumb-founded! How could this be? I thought back to these emails and the convention I'd attended a few weeks before, and added those experiences to my current question: *Is everyone staring at me?* I began to second-guess everything I was doing. Did I get it wrong? Was *I* the reason everyone was staring at me? To answer this question, I had to go back in time to a promise I made to God in May 2013, after dinner with my friend Elizabeth.

Elizabeth and I had been friends for more than twenty years. She is probably the smartest woman I know. She is a pharmacist who has branched out to managing hospitals and writing books on leadership and business reform. She called me two weeks before my birthday saying she was going to be in Oakland, about an hour south of our home in Fairfield, and she wanted to take me out for a birthday dinner at a nice restaurant in Jack London Square. We had not seen each other in several years, and I was excited to catch up.

I will never forget that dinner. We were sitting in a booth looking out over the marina. We had ordered and were enjoying our time. All of a sudden, my sweet, Nigerian friend got a very serious look on her face and began to bust my chops. She pointed her finger at my face across the table and told me that I was wasting my God-given talent by not speaking and blogging.

As her robust, Nigerian voice got louder and louder, the waitress finally came over and asked if everything was all right. I remember telling the waitress that my friend loved me and was trying to convince me to do something we both knew it was time for me to do—get back to blogging and speaking. Elizabeth always believed that this was God's plan for my life. Through prayer and encouragement, she was my biggest supporter. She repeatedly encouraged me that night to "stop wasting your God-given gifts and get back to the task!"

For a period of ten years while my children were growing up, I had a ministry called Homebase Ministries. It started out as a challenge by Pastor Greg—the same Greg who became a friend and now is my friend and therapist. He had challenged me to start a ministry for wives whose husbands were pastors in California. The purpose was to enlist other wives to pray for them and to offer a safe place where they could share. The ministry quickly grew and began to reach women, not just ministry wives, all over the world. My blogging opened up opportunities to travel all over the country to teach and speak. I loved Homebase Ministries and all that I did there, but when my husband left the ministry to work for the foundation, someone said I could no longer know what it felt like to be a pastor's wife. I had gotten out, and they were still stuck. Being told I could no longer relate made me feel rejected again.

I wish I could say that I didn't let my fear of rejection and not being good enough get in the way, but I happily walked away from Homebase Ministries and closed the door on that ministry when we moved to Fresno. Bill was no longer a pastor and that meant I was no longer a blogger or speaker. As far as I was concerned, I would never blog, speak, or teach again. Instead I became a successful event planner. And when my husband returned to ministry after working at the foundation and I became a pastor's wife again, I was content to continue my safe job of event planning. I was good at it, and there was no rejection. I never looked back until that dinner with Elizabeth.

As I drove home that night from my birthday dinner, I began to pray. I told God that I knew He had allowed me to stop, but I asked Him why and asked Him if Elizabeth was correct in telling me it was time to begin again. God told me that He allowed me to stop because He needed me to learn a few things. He needed me to be fully committed to transparency and total honesty. I remember telling God out loud in my car that I was willing. I promised Him that my life would be an open book and that I would be transparent and honest. If He could use any of the experiences I had been through in my life to encourage others, then I was His girl. I immediately began work on designing a new website, and over the next few months I got everything set up. On January 1, 2014, I launched Carole's Journey and began the journey of blogging and teaching again.

Since that night in 2013 when I promised God to be transparent with my life for Him, I had never looked back. Well, until four years later, when once again I faced my rejection at the convention by the pastor suggesting I was a life-weary, broken-down, miserable woman and the email asking me why I was airing my dirty laundry in public. My promise to be an open book and to allow God to use my life circumstances made me wonder if I would have changed my mind had I known what the future held.

I came home from that 2017 convention asking God if I had heard Him correctly. Had Elizabeth been right in challenging me to get back to work? Did I make a mistake by being so transparent? Was I airing my dirty laundry? Was I a broken-down, miserable, life-weary woman who everyone was staring at? God's answer to me was this: *You heard me correctly! I am proud of how brave you have been. Keep trusting, keep sharing, and keep choosing joy. Your story will help so many people.*

Time and experience have been the teacher for me in finding an answer to wondering if everybody is staring at me. The answer is yes, but as the painful circumstances continued, and the days turned into months and years, I discovered that some of those starers were also believing a bold-faced lie, and it's a doozy. The lie is this: when our lives are perfect, we are blessed by God, but when we have trials, there must be a hidden sin and God must be angry at us. I knew this lie existed, and I have experienced it firsthand. Someone asked me what Bill's hidden sin was. Another person asked me what Bill did to make God so mad. I realize now how many Christians buy into this falsehood.

Here is the truth: there is no hidden sin. Bill is an incredible, loving husband, father, and grandfather who suffers from a genetic, chemical imbalance that produces anxiety. This anxiety causes him to try and control everything to relieve the pain. When he can't control life, he sinks into a depression. Without medication, suicidal thoughts flood his mind, and he starts thinking about killing himself to escape the pain. It is a cycle I have watched him go through many times over the last four years. I realize now that he has struggled with anxiety for his entire life, and somewhere along the way, his system could no longer handle the pressure this cycle puts on him. When that happens, he crashes into depression and wants to kill himself. There is no sin, there is nothing Bill has done to deserve this, and our lives have been full of God taking care of us during the scary times of searching for answers.

I have learned some other very practical things over the last five years. I am stronger than I thought I was, and God has been preparing me my entire life for this moment. Having to take charge of my family and household as a young child taught me to navigate financial and medical choices I need to make now. Interestingly enough, my wonderful husband also helped in the preparation I would need for his crisis. I came into our marriage with huge rejection issues, and Bill helped me overcome these fears and learn to trust again. Bill was my pastor and my favorite speaker. As I sat under his teaching over many years, his messages helped me grow in my faith and develop a deep, personal relationship with God. I learned how to trust Bill and God. I got so close to God, that in the crisis of the moment, I drew even closer to Him, talking to Him, screaming at Him, expecting Him to answer—and He did!

Another thing I learned is that isolation is not the answer. It seems natural to crawl into the bed of life and bury under the covers so no one or nothing can hurt us. It feels safe, warm, and protected. Isolating for a time can be helpful, but it's vital to get out of bed and rejoin life. Isolating means losing. We can shut people out because we don't want to get hurt, but when we isolate, we also shut out the people who can help us.

Another hard truth is that even the Christians we consider family or close friends can become the opposition, hurting us by misquoting Scripture and handing out judgment. They begin to question our actions, even though we tell them we are following God's direction. Some will walk away and abandon us at the moment we need them most. Facing this opposition has taught me to continue to believe the truth of Scripture and focus on how God has worked. I then become persistent in my choice to rely on God, believing Him above all else, knowing from experience He will never abandon me. Believe it or not, a few of the dumb things that people have said or shared with me have been some of the most helpful things. Yep, you read that correctly. A few of these dumb, painful things have caused me to take a hard look at myself. I discovered that when life gets painful enough, I listen, evaluate, and make changes if needed. I step up, look inside, and evaluate. I am not a broken-down, miserable, life-weary woman who finally turned back to God. I have been glued to God's side since before Bill's breakdown, and I moved even closer to Him when it happened. I am not airing my dirty laundry for all the world to see. I am showing people that God cares and shows up for us when we have a need!

Let me revisit this question again: *Is everybody staring at me?* Yes, people are always watching me. People are always watching all of us. Our entire lives are lived with people staring and paying attention to what we say and do. The Scripture in James says, "You know that under pressure, your faith-life is forced into the open and shows its true colors." I am realizing this was God's exact plan all along. What I had hoped to accomplish—by promising God I would be open, honest, transparent, and available to use the circumstances of my life—has happened. I want people to see that we can choose joy when life is messy. I want people to see that God is a personal God who always shows up. I want my life to be a story that draws people in who cheer me on, yet wonder how I'm not flat on the floor in a puddle.

I want people to watch—to stare—before, during, and after the mess. I've gotten my wish; everyone is staring, and my story points them directly toward God. You can't know me without knowing that I am a Daddy's girl, and my Daddy is God!

# 7

## God's Gift to Us Is in the Trials

*Consider it a sheer gift, friends.*
James 1:2

**My TV career started early.** For my fifth birthday, my mom arranged for me and some friends to be on TV. I lived in the Sacramento area, and there was a local TV show called *Captain Delta*, which I watched every morning. For my birthday that year, my mom arranged for my party to be held on the set of the *Captain Delta* show. At one point during the show, Captain Delta asked me, "What are you getting for your birthday?" My answer, "A baby sister." This was in 1963, before sonograms and gender reveal parties. My mom was expecting a baby at any moment, and somehow, I knew it would be a girl. When I came home from the show that day, my mom had gone into labor and was at the hospital delivering the baby. The baby would technically not be born until two days after my birthday, but my favorite birthday gift to this day is my sister Trish. We have always tried to celebrate our birthdays together and I can count on her to give me the perfect gift every year.

Gift giving can be a challenge, but these days when you get married or have a baby, you register for gifts and make lists of items you would like to receive. These wish lists make it easy for those who love you to give you exactly what you want. In our family we make long, detailed lists when it comes to gift giving. Trials, challenges, or messes have never shown up on anyone's wish list.

Even with lists, we have all gotten that gift at one time or another—the one we didn't ask for and can't use. What do we do? The solution is usually to hide it in a closet or drawer, return it, or quietly regift it to someone else. Sometimes we discover that our unwanted gift is the perfect gift for someone else. It might even be something they have on their gift wish list. What if we could regift a trial or a mess? I have wanted out of the trials and the messiness of my life so badly, but I never once thought, *I wish I could give this to someone else.*

If you were to read the first few words of James 1:2, "Consider it a sheer gift, friends," would you like me think of receiving a snuggly, cute kitten; a wiggly, adorable puppy; a pony; or a trip to Disneyland? The Message translation says "a sheer gift," and the NIV translation says, "pure joy." The word *friends* makes it seem like someone close to you, someone who loves you and thinks you're special, is giving you the most beautiful, wonderful gift.

One of the hardest lessons I have learned from my messy life is that God sees trials differently than we do. He sees them as gifts to help us grow. When I read the words James wrote, "Consider it a sheer gift, friends," he is talking about trials being gifts. As I sit and look back at the trials, the messy parts of my life, I would never find myself using the words *sheer gift* or *joy* to describe the pain and fear I experience. I have screamed at God more than once, telling Him I don't want the trial. *Really, can I please just give this wonderful trial gift back?* I wouldn't even want to regift it to anyone else, not even my worst enemy. I know this sounds irreverent, but the beautiful thing about God is that He can take our anger. He hears our words, knows our hearts, and is lovingly patient.

The last time I found myself screaming these words to God was on a plane to one of my favorite places in the world—Maui.

God used a trip to Maui to help me understand how He uses trials in our lives. And when they come, He is right there speaking. All we have to do is listen.

My perfect gift, one I consider a *sheer gift* of *pure joy* is the island of Maui. It is by far one of my favorite places in the world. The island has everything I want in a vacation—sun, sand, relaxation, and humpback whales. I have vacationed in Hawaii forty times. My favorite island is Maui, and our daughter, Kate, got married on Wailea Beach on Maui during one of those visits. There are many things I love about the island. My favorite way to start every morning is by sitting on the sand, watching the sun rise over the ocean with a cup of coffee in hand. Another activity I enjoy is whale watching. I love the feel of the wind and the spray of the ocean as the boat glides across the water. There is great adventure in searching the horizon for whales and excitement when I finally spot one. If you want to give me the perfect gift, give me a trip to Maui, where I seem to have no problems, nor a care in the world. There is relaxation and nothing but sun, sand, and fun.

Our longtime friends invited us to join them on their island vacation in 2019, and my excitement was immeasurable. I had not had a real vacation in so long, and this trip was the perfect gift at the perfect time. You might say I was experiencing the sheer joy of this gift. God used this trip from the moment our plane took off to teach me about the joy of trials and listening to Him. The trip started with the scariest plane ride I've ever had, I actually wanted to drop to my knees and kiss the ground of the airport after getting off the plane. I have never experienced turbulence like that flight. The turbulence was so severe, it was like a roller coaster up and down and back and forth, seemingly all at the same time! At one point, with tears quietly running down my cheeks as we flew over the middle of the ocean, I closed my eyes and said, *Really, just really? God, is this how I am going to start my first real vacation in three years?* My next prayer was, *Really, God, is this is how my life is going to end?* His answer? Silence.

As the plane continued to shake and dip, I remembered my "When Life Gets Scary" playlist on my phone. I opened my phone to that list and hit shuffle. The music began to play, and I couldn't believe the first song that started playing was one that has comforted me so many times over the last three years. Familiar words began to calm my nerves as I sat with my eyes closed listening to the singer remind me that God is my hope and that I should trust Him. He gives me strength, and "it is well with my soul," as the song states. My mind blocked out everything else, and a quiet calm came over me.

As I sat there with the plane still rocking from the turbulence, eyes closed, I began to replay the events of my life from the last three years. It was like watching a movie of my life—all my fears, all my hurts, all my questions—and I realized there was something very familiar in each scene. From the very beginning, even before my life took this crazy path and before Bill began to struggle with the anxiety, depression, and suicidal thoughts, God was there, *and* He still is. Yes, He is. Then I heard something else familiar. These words. The ones God spoke into my heart early one morning more than three years ago. *I've got you, Princess. I'm right here, and no matter what happens, you will be okay. I will be here to walk with you and to hold you close and to carry you when it gets too hard. You must fight through the fears and trust Me!* The plane was still rocking and rolling, but my fear was gone. Then God spoke some new words into my heart at that moment. He said, *I've got you baby girl, rest in Me.* And I did.

The trial of the turbulence reminded me that once again God has a plan and He was and is right there with me. I experienced one of the bumpiest and hardest plane landings ever, but we finally landed in Maui. As I stepped off the plane, I deeply breathed in the tropical warm and humid air, and I gazed at the beach off in the distance. I whispered to God, *I am here, thank You for creating this beautiful island.* We were still a bit shaken from the rough trip and landing as we picked up our luggage, but as we climbed into the Jeep we had rented, the sense of adventure, laughter, and smiles returned. We were on vacation, and the plane ride was all but forgotten for now.

Very early the next morning, I sat in the Starbucks I had discovered in our hotel. I had my coffee and was looking out the window, waiting for the sun to come up so I could venture out onto the sand. I began to process my emotions from the plane ride the day before, when I feared that the plane might have crashed. I was angry my vacation had started this way, as I was already mentally exhausted. I had a choice to make. I had to decide whether or not I was going to let my terror of the plane ride and my anger and exhaustion ruin my entire vacation. My fear of getting back on a plane seven days from then threatened to keep me from enjoying the rest of the trip, and I knew that if I didn't let go of my anger, I was never going to relax enough to get over the exhaustion.

I thought back to a lesson I learned when Bill came home from the psychiatric hospital. If I truly believed that God has a plan, and I am a part of that plan, then I can turn my fear of the trial into an anticipation of the journey. I looked out the window to see the sun just barely rising over the ocean. There were so many adventures waiting in that beautiful horizon. My lesson on listening to God and finding joy in the trials was going to help me set my fears and anger aside, and I was going to enjoy the remainder of our vacation. So once again, I chose joy.

I picked up my coffee and walked out to the beach. I sat down in the sand as close to the water as I could without getting wet. As I watched the waves lap on the sand in front of me, the sun was rising in the sky over the mountains in the distance, creating a beautiful, colorful sunrise, and I began to praise God for His gift of Maui. God was so close to me at that moment, I could feel His presence in the creation surrounding me.

Enjoying the moment and resting in God, I heard Him say, *I love you, my sweet girl. The trip may have started off rough, but you are here. I've got you; get ready for the coming adventures.* I stood up to go back to my hotel room, and as I turned to take one last look at the sunrise, a huge whale breached right offshore. Tears rolled down my cheeks. God knew how much joy I would get from this, the perfect gift at that moment.

We spent our first few vacation days on the beach, enjoying the sun and snorkeling. I got to experience my favorite adventure already, having gone out in a boat to whale watch. It was Bill's turn for his favorite adventure. He loves driving the backroads of the island in a four-wheel-drive Jeep. I can recall many of those trips: my kids driving for the first time in a riverbed; my daughter telling us there was an "opotion" (she meant opposition) in the car when her father wanted to go down a steep hill over huge boulders; my friend being fearful of that same hill a few years later, saying, "Stop this car right now! I am getting out if you keep going this direction." There had been so many four-wheel-driving memories, I would have told you there could not possibly be another new one added. Well, I would have been wrong, and God had a lesson to teach me.

The south side of the island is a very remote place. The rental car businesses recommend that you don't drive there, because it can take a very long time for a tow truck to come and pick you up if your car breaks down. I have seen tow trucks pulling multiple cars on these backroads. On day three of our vacation, we set out on our four-wheel-drive adventure on the south side of the island. Our plan was to make our way along this road to one of Bill's favorite snorkel spots, enjoy a picnic on a black sand beach by a beautiful old church, and finally take a four-mile hike to a waterfall. It was a day packed with fun, and a delay would not be welcome.

Our friend Marc was driving, and he pulled off at a beautiful spot so we could stretch our legs and take some photos of the gorgeous shoreline. We took our pictures and got back into the Jeep. He turned the key and nothing. The dashboard was lighting up, so it couldn't be the battery. He tried everything. The guys got out and lifted the hood to look at the engine and tried starting the car again. Nothing.

Marc decided it was time to call the rental company, and Bill flagged down a tow truck he saw coming. The tow-truck driver gave him the phone number of the towing company because he was already loaded up with two other cars. As the tow-truck driver drove away, he told Bill, "I hope you have food and water; you're going to be here awhile." Although we were parked in a beautiful location, we couldn't enjoy the view anymore because we were stuck.

My thoughts immediately went to, *Really, God, couldn't we please have gotten through today without a trial?* As I watched Marc on hold with the rental car company, I realized we still had cell service. So I pulled out my phone and searched, "My 2018 Jeep Wrangler won't start." I got a long list of sites and videos, and I clicked on one video, having a strange feeling it could provide the answer. But after a few seconds, I turned it off, deciding it was a stupid idea. As I sat there, I had the nagging thought that perhaps this video really could help. Marc was still on hold and we were still stuck, so what did I have to lose? I picked up my phone, found the video, and began to watch it again.

The man in the video explained how to reset something. He kept saying, "This is probably the issue. Get under the hood and find this fuse in this box." I jumped out of the car, lifted the hood of the Jeep, located the fuse box, and started the video over again. At this moment, a man on a motorcycle drove up to me and said, "This doesn't look good, man." I laugh now as I remember his face and think about how ridiculous I must have looked, leaning over the engine of the car and watching a video on my phone. The guys told him we had it under control, and he drove away, shaking his head. I opened the fuse box, started the video again, and located the fuse.

Bill now joined me under the hood, and Marc watched the fun. I knew this was going to be the answer. My excitement grew as the video said to pull a certain fuse and replace it after thirty seconds, and that would allow the car to start. We all held our breath as Marc got behind the wheel. He put the key in the ignition, and *vroom*. We all yelled with excitement as the car started. We got back in the car and had a decision to make. Were we going to continue our adventure, or turn back in fear of the car stalling again? We had barely started on our excursion. Were we going to trust and keep on the path, or return to the hotel in fear?

It was not a unanimous vote, but we pulled back onto the road in the direction of finishing our adventure. It turned out to be a fun day, and we are all glad that we had the experience to add to our Maui memories. Did you catch what I just wrote? If we had turned back that day because we were afraid of getting stuck again, we would have missed the rest of our amazing adventure, not to mention the crazy story to add to our Maui four-wheel-drive memories. We have had many laughs about the solution, and I have been dubbed the person you most want to get stuck with, as long as I have cell service and my phone.

Finding joy in my messy life has been a process. It is a life of trusting God and His incredible adventure for us. When Bill's anxiety gets out of control, when I am afraid that his suicidal thoughts will return, when I am exhausted from the trials coming at me from all directions, I cry out to God. My first response might be to question, but then I turn back to the truth I have learned from James 1:2: "Consider it a sheer gift, friends." I remember that He sees trials differently than we do. They are His gift to help us grow and to teach us to trust Him. Instead of asking God, *Can I please give this gift back?* I stop and change my focus: *Thank You, God, for lessons I am learning from this gift.*

When I choose to move my focus from the fear of the trial to the adventure of the journey, I can see that He has a plan and He is usually already speaking to me. How many times does God give us the answer but we are too scared, think it's too silly, or stop trusting that He is actually giving us the answer? We want lightning to strike. We want God to speak in a loud, booming voice. We want clear instructions. The Bible tells us in Job 38:1 that God spoke to Job through a violent storm. In Deuteronomy 4:12, God spoke through a fire, and in 1 Kings 19:13, God spoke to Elijah in a quiet whisper. In this age of technology, sometimes God speaks through a cell phone and a YouTube video. I am so glad that I was listening.

# 8

## Mastering Mental Gymnastics

*Let it do its work . . .*
James 1:4

**When you love and care for someone who suffers from** mental illness, everything becomes about them. Their symptoms, medication, doctor and psychiatrist appointments, how they feel, what to say, what not to say—they become the center of your universe. Life can become exhausting and overwhelming, and it can be easy to get lost and stop taking care of yourself when this is the reality you live with, especially if you were not very good at it to begin with. As soon as you stop taking care of yourself, your own survival is in jeopardy. There is a companion illness that affects those who care for loved ones struggling with mental illness: caregiver burnout.

Caregiver burnout has manifested itself in me through anger, tiredness, insomnia, guilt, shame, overreacting, overeating, isolating, and cutting back on activities I love to do. Caregiver burnout affects each person differently. For me, I have found that it is critical to constantly look at my emotions; I call it taking my emotional temperature.

In James 1:4 he writes, "Let it do its work," referring to the tests and challenges that cause pressure. As the caregiver for someone who struggles with mental illness, I have learned there is a delicate balance between the pressure that can help spiritually mature me or potentially destroy me. Unfortunately there is more help for the struggler than the caregiver. It is time for that to change.

I have learned that my husband's mental illness is a cycle. He does great for a few days or a few weeks or even a few months, and I find myself telling family and friends, "Bill is doing so much better. His medication is working, and I think we are out of danger." Then *wham*, the cycle starts all over again. I don't know why I am gobsmacked every time it happens again. Yes, *gobsmacked*; it means "utterly astonished, astounded.⁴" Life can feel like I'm on a hamster wheel, and I'm running, running, running, and then I stop. I find myself exhausted and out of breath and right back where I started, dealing once again with pain, disappointment, fear, and rejection. Some days I wake up and tell God, *I am just done! I can't do this anymore. I quit!*

I remember one day in particular when Bill's anxiety and depression were raging. He was trying to control everything, and I was not cooperating, so I was naturally to blame for his pain. Normally, if I walk away for a few minutes, he will calm down. I had walked away and was sitting in the back room at my computer. In a moment of rash anger, Bill walked to the doorway, put his hands on his hips, and told me I had two choices: I could have him pack his stuff and leave, because he believed that is what I really wanted, or he could move all my stuff from our bedroom into the back room and I could live there for the rest of my life. I looked at him, saw how much pain he was in, and I told him, "Babe, you have no idea what I want. You are going to have to choose, because I don't like either option." He stomped his foot, turned away, and as he walked off said, "There you go, trying to control the world again."

A few minutes later I could hear him behind me as he started walking in and out of the room. I knew he was moving my stuff from our room into the back room I was working in. I turned and watched as he carefully placed and organized all my stuff in the closet. When he was done, he went back into our bedroom and closed the door. I found myself ugly crying over the disappointment. I was being rejected, and my healing heart was broken again.

On that morning, I hit my wall. I felt alone and the rejection took me down the road of guilt and shame. These are two symptoms of severe caregiver's burnout. I began to question, *What did I do? Should I have done something differently? What's wrong with me?* I had picked up and started carrying around some guilt and shame that didn't belong to me. This guilt told me that I wasn't enough for him and that I couldn't help him. I then began to question if perhaps I was really the one with the problem and if I was actually the one who was really sick. Next I went down the road of shame, wondering what people were going to say, beating myself up for not having enough faith, and scared of people finding out more of our mess.

Jack and his family were arriving the next day for a visit, and my mom was arriving as well. I was going to refuse to hide that he had moved me into the guest room. Jack and Lee would sleep on the couches next door, and my mom would have to stay in my grand-daughters' room upstairs. I would have to explain why. My guilt, shame, and rejection opened up a painful wound, and I jumped back on that hamster wheel, trying to outrun my hurt yet again.

As I sat looking around my new bedroom, my eyes went to a note on the window with John 3:16 written on it. The words read, "This is how much God loved Carole, He gave his son, his one and only son for her. And this is why, so Carole need not be destroyed. By believing in Jesus, Carole can have a whole and lasting life." I was reminded again that my true identity was found when I met Christ as a sixteen-year-old and *all* my sins were forgiven—past, present, and future.

God sees me through the shed blood of Jesus; therefore, I can make a mistake without being a mistake. No guilt or shame needed. We can replace guilt and shame with restoration. There is nothing

I have ever done or will ever do that will make God reject or stop loving me. Nothing will take away His restoration. This is true for *all* of us. God also reminds me that my husband suffers from mental illness, and I have no reason to pick up the guilt or shame. Will I put them down and trust Him with my fears, pain, rejection?

I decided that morning I was going to sit and have a cup of coffee with my wounds. I was going to examine them and really see what they were saying to me. So I opened my "When Life Gets Scary" playlist, hit shuffle play, put a coffee pod in my coffee maker, pushed brew, and took a deep breath.

As the coffee dripped into my favorite cup, I began to think about this current rejection. I then added the rejections of the past few years and topped it off with the memories of my abusive, alcoholic father all those years before. Once again, tears started welling up in my eyes. I asked myself these questions:

> *Why am I still attaching guilt or shame to this pesky wound?* Why do I keep tripping up at this exact point every time? Why do guilt and shame creep back in and attack my sense of identity? Why do I start to focus on the lies guilt and shame are telling me? Why do I go back to that wheel of running and running and running?

One of my favorite worship songs was playing in the background, and the words caught my attention. They were about how I am much stronger and braver than I know. I didn't need to be afraid because God and I would face it all together. I grabbed my coffee from the machine and again realized that I was not alone; I didn't have to face my wounds alone. God was right there with me. I walked outside and imagined that He was sitting there in my garden enjoying a cup of coffee with me. As we sat sipping coffee, my thoughts transitioned to an important truth I learned about guilt and shame. I immediately took a deep breath and wiped the tears from my eyes. I stopped beating myself up and got off that wheel.

When I feel guilt, I perceive I did something bad (sin). When I feel shame, I perceive there is something wrong with me—essentially I am bad (identity). Do you notice the difference? I *did* something bad versus I *am* bad. Or to be clearer, I *made* a mistake versus I *am* a mistake. In my current circumstance, I had not done anything bad, so there was no need for guilt. I had not sinned or made any mistakes. There was definitely nothing wrong with me either, so no shame was needed. I was not a mistake!

I put my coffee cup down, walked back into my new bedroom, picked up my journal, and walked back out to my garden. As I sat in the sun, I opened the journal and wrote the words "mental gymnastics" in big, bold letters. When dealing with my husband's mental illness—his anxiety, depression, and need for control—it becomes a sort of mental gymnastics for both of us. I think about watching an Olympic gymnast compete with body twists, turns, and tumbles. My mind does the same thing with words, feelings, and emotions, as I try to make sense out of something that makes no sense. My mind does mental gymnastics as I try to take on responsibility for fixing Bill, as I get angry when he blames me, as I feel guilt and shame because I think this mess is all my fault, as I forget about restoration and tell myself I don't deserve this. Back to that squeaky hamster wheel I go, running, running, and running. I tell God, *Something has to change.*

His answer to me, *You are so right, Princess, you do. You need to change. Now, get off this hamster wheel and get to work.*

An Olympic gymnast trains for years before competing. My training for the mental gymnastics of Bill's mental illness has been the four-plus decades we have spent loving each other. We made a vow to God saying we will love each other and spend the rest of our lives together, and we have a beautiful family to show for it. I started thinking about the changes I would need to make to my training in order to train, survive, and master the mental gymnastics I face each day.

On the page in my journal underneath "mental gymnastics," I wrote the words "training," "surviving," and "mastering." It was important for me to understand the definitions of those three words, so I looked them up online in my phone and wrote the definitions in my journal next to each word.

> Training—"The activity of learning a new skill or behavior."[5]
> Surviving—"Continuing to live in spite of a difficult circumstances."[6]
> Mastering—"To gain control of or overcome."[7]

As I sat staring at the words and definitions, I decided to write the definitions down on sticky notes. After I was done having coffee with God that morning, I put the sticky notes on the window in my new bedroom. As I stared at each word and definition, God began to show me how He had already been helping me master mental gymnastics.

Much like how an Olympic gymnast's training changes with time and experience, my training had to change when mental illness became a part of our lives. I had to learn new skills and behaviors. I found myself evaluating every corner of my life. My son taught me the first lesson on how my training needed to change.

I was driving back to Jack's house after visiting Bill in the psychiatric hospital the first time, asking God, *What do I do now?* As soon as I walked into the house, Jack told me that he and Lee were taking CJ to Disneyland the next day, and he insisted that I go with them. I looked at him and said, "I can't go to Disneyland; your dad is in a psychiatric hospital. Do you realize what is going on?" I love that he smiled and gently encouraged me, "Yes, Mom, I am completely aware of what's going on, and you're going to Disneyland tomorrow." I fully intended to refuse, and then my love for Disneyland and for CJ changed my mind, and I said, "Yes, I will go."

We had a wonderful day. I was able to relax and enjoy myself. Our family had annual passes, and trips to Disneyland were common for us. I found moments that day on my favorite ride, Pirates of the Caribbean, or riding Little Mermaid with CJ, where I was able to put my fear aside and laugh. A few days later Kate and her family arrived for Thanksgiving week, and we went to Disneyland for two more days. Each time we went, I had a few weepy moments where I would stop to think about what was going on. Bill was still in the hospital, and he should be with us. Then one of my grandchildren would pull me onto a ride, or Minnie Mouse would walk by and wave, and I would forget again for a few moments and find the fun and comfort of being in my favorite place with my family. Yes, my husband was in a psychiatric hospital and I went to Disneyland. Don't you think this sounds like a great title for a country song?

During one of my weepy sessions, while standing in line for a ride, Jack made a comment to me that changed my perspective and the way I trained. I was crying as we stood in line for Splash Mountain, and he said, "Mom, you can't change what is going on with Dad. You have to take care of yourself, and right now you are here with us and with your grandchildren." Sweeping his arms out, he said, "Enjoy this moment. You need to take care of you, and we will figure out what to do later." I smiled and hugged him. He was right, and when we got off the ride, I bought Mickey ice cream bars for everyone and a new Minnie Mouse sweatshirt for me. Every time I put that sweatshirt on, I remember Jack's words.

Self-care became a critical part of my training that day. I began to make sure I ate healthy, got enough sleep, and exercised. I began to make sure that routine visits for massages, hair, and nails were calendared. And I began to pray for a new therapist to talk to. My training became: take care of me, enjoy this moment, and figure out what to do later.

When gymnasts want to quit or become injured, they have a coach who steps up and gives them a pep talk. My daughter gave me the pep talk on survival that helped me continue to live in spite of a difficult circumstance. She taught me that I needed to find something to do.

It was early January 2017 and a cold, foggy Bakersfield morning. We had been home for a few weeks from Deryl and Brenda's house. Bill was now enrolled in an intensive, outpatient program (IOP) in town, and he was still struggling with anxiety, depression, and suicidal thoughts. We had joined Valley Baptist Church, and I was settling into a daily routine.

I would wake up, get Bill his medication and a bowl of cereal, and sit by the electric fireplace in our living room with a cup of coffee. I would then get Bill up and we would drive to his IOP class, where I would sit in the car reading for hours until he was done. We would grab lunch on the way back to the house, Bill would nap, and I would read by the fire until Kate and her family came home. Sometimes I would help her fix dinner, then Bill would lay on the couch, and I'd sit by the fire watching a movie until it was time for bed.

For the first two weeks we were home, I was in a fog, and these were constants that kept me going: his medication, a bowl of cereal, coffee, my fireplace, IOP, a good book, lunch, another fire, more coffee, dinner, another fire, a movie, and bed. Every day was exactly the same.

One Saturday evening, Kate came in, sat down, and said, "Mom, I know you don't really like to work with children, but I need someone to help with checking kids in at church on Sunday mornings. Would you be willing to help? You could start tomorrow." As she sat there with her big eyes staring at me, I intended to say "No!" But instead I heard, "Of course, Princess, what time do I need to be there?" She had just gotten me to take my first step of survival—something to do to help me get back to living. She then told me I needed some fresh flowers to add some color to my living room, and how about some candles?

Once the initial shock wore off, I became really good at training and surviving. I volunteered each Sunday morning, checking children in. I bought a Nespresso machine, added some candles, and kept fresh flowers in a vase in my living room. I created a space where I could enjoy a cup of coffee, sit by my fireplace, watch a movie, and feel good. It was a place that made me smile every time I walked into the room. The tension, fear, anger, and discouragement melted away whenever I walked into that room. It was a perfect place to curl up in a blanket, turn on the fire, and sip a cup of coffee.

Kate wasn't done though. A few weeks into January, she had her mother-in-law, Cindy, call and invite me to a Bible study she led each week on Wednesday mornings. Cindy told me that she knew Deryl had introduced me to his friend Jane, who was a member of the church in Bakersfield. When we moved back home, Deryl had called Jane and asked her to look out for me. Between Kate, Cindy, and Jane, they got me to commit to the eight-week Bible study. Jane was my table leader. I can't even tell you what we studied. Bill would go with me and sit in the car because he didn't want to stay home alone. I would walk in at the last minute and usually leave early before the discussion, but I was getting out of the house and meeting other women.

I had to make the effort because training and survival are about choosing. Choosing to take care of yourself, choosing to enjoy the moment, and choosing to live. About week four of the Bible study, I began to feel comfortable with the women at my table and started staying for the small-group discussion time. I discovered that several of the women at my table were going through some pretty traumatic things, and I found myself sharing about my situation. As I opened up, I found acceptance, support, love, and encouragement. I wasn't alone anymore. Kate was right—I needed something to do.

Back in my garden, there was a moment when a hummingbird came to the feeder above my head. He dropped down and hovered right in front of my face, staring at me for a few moments. I felt like he was reminding me to smile and enjoy creation. I sat and sipped my coffee, took a deep breath, and remembered God was right there.

He is my coach, and when I want to quit, I go back to His Word. I started remembering all the ways He had helped me get this far, then I closed my journal and decided to sit and enjoy watching the hummingbirds for a little while longer. I chose to find joy at that moment of calm and quiet. In a few minutes, I would get up, stick my notes on the window and put sheets on my new bed. I had no idea how long this was going to last, how long I would be in this bedroom, but I knew that my coach would walk through this with me. I have His restoration so I would not get back on that hamster wheel of guilt and shame. I would not feel rejected. I would not quit! I smiled as I imagined God holding up a cardboard sign with a perfect ten on it.

# 9

## Learning to Live with What I Have

*So you become mature and well-developed, not deficient in any way.*
James 1:4

Imani is the most exotic, beautiful Bengal cat, and I am her human. I met her when she was ten weeks old. I have always loved Bengal cats and dreamed of one day owning one. My friend Kelsey has two and told me Bakersfield has one of the top breeders of Bengals in the world. I wanted to meet the cats and know more about them, so I made an appointment to meet the breeders and their cats so I could ask questions. I had no intention of getting a kitten that day. The afternoon of our appointment arrived, and I was to meet the breeders at their home. I was so excited as I walked into the dining room and saw tiny bundles of spotted fur rolling around on the floor, chasing each other, and tackling each other. I could hear them practicing the distinct chirp that is the Bengal cat's natural communication.

I sat down on the floor so I could see under the dining room table. As I watched the kittens play, the breeder told me there was only one kitten available. "Most of these kittens you are watching are twelve weeks old and will be going to their new homes this week.

The one kitten available is from the ten-week-old litter," and she pointed down the hallway where tiny eyes were watching me from the doorway. She said, "These kittens won't be available for another two weeks." She then said, "The one kitten available is very brave and loves to play out here with this older litter."

She directed me to look under the chair in front of me and handed me a stick with some ribbon on the end and told me to shake it on the floor under the chair. As I placed the stick on the ground, a tiny kitten with bright green eyes appeared. She looked at me and we locked eyes. While the tiny kitten and I were having a who-will-blink-first contest, the breeder said, "You found her; that is the available kitten." My heart swelled with love, and from that moment, I was her person. The breeder could see that we were meant for each other and began to negotiate the purchase. I had promised Bill I would not make a commitment that day, but I was already in love, so it was hard to choke out the words. "I need to think about it," I said. She told me that someone was coming the next day to look at the kitten, and without a deposit, she couldn't hold her for me.

As I walked out of the house, it was hard not to cry. Bill could see how much I loved that kitten, and while we were eating lunch in a restaurant about a mile down the road, he said, "Call them and let them know we want her. We will go get the deposit and bring it back in an hour." I made the call and then opened my phone to begin searching for the perfect name. I wanted the name to be Swahili, so I began to search for a girl's name. I found an interesting name, and when I read the meaning, "Faith, belief, and confidence," I knew that my new kitten's name was *Imani*. We went to the bank, picked up the deposit, and took the money to the breeder. As I signed the contract, I picked her up and snuggled her close. I told the breeder her name, and she wrote it on the contract. I would be able to take Imani home in two weeks.

Once we got her home, she became the princess of the house. It only took her a few hours to settle in. Bengals are not lap cats and usually don't snuggle, but from day one, Imani's favorite nap spot was my lap. She stretches out and takes over my lap, just like she had already taken over my heart.

She has so much energy that sometimes she gets wild. The hair on her back stands up, her tail puffs out, she will stare at me with her back arched, and then all of a sudden she starts running up and down the hall. She runs in circles, and sometimes she does a somersault. She makes me laugh, brings me so much joy, and even teaches me life lessons.

I couldn't believe she was mine, and I wondered why she was not chosen to be a show cat. Imani has the perfect markings, personality, and pedigree to become a champion show cat. She even comes from a long line of world-class Bengals. The breeder had suggested the veterinarian they use, so when I took Imani in for her next round of shots, the doctor would be the one to answer that question. When he walked into the room, he had a file on her already. He looked at her, then at the file, and said, "I remember this kitten. She is the one with a deformity." I looked at him in shock and somehow got out the word, "Deformity?" He pointed out the problem, and I breathed a sigh of relief.

A tiny tip of her left ear was missing. A piece so small, that unless you knew to look for it, you would never notice it was missing. This missing tip of her left ear makes it impossible for her to follow in her family footsteps. She can't be shown or bred because of this very small missing tip of her ear. The veterinarian said, "No one knows if she was born that way or if something happened when she was a very young kitten. We just know it is missing." I realized that this small missing tip of her ear had changed the path of her life. Instead of traveling the world as an expensive show cat, she came to live with me as a very spoiled and pampered pet.

Sometimes I look at her and wonder, *what if?* What would her life have been like if the tip of her ear was not gone? Was she missing out on something in life because of that defect? Then I find myself so happy about the missing part of her ear because she gets to live with me. I begin to wonder if am I being selfish in my happiness?

Imani has taught me many lessons, the first being that I had to stop asking what-if questions for good. What if I could fix her ear? What if I could restore her charmed Bengal life? I can't. It is impossible to fix her ear and restore her destiny as a champion show cat. She seems pretty happy with the life she has with me, and I am thrilled she is mine. I decided it was time to stop asking those questions about her life and just enjoy my beautiful cat. God continued to challenge me to use the lesson from Imani and apply it to my own life. He was not done teaching me about the what-if questions I was still asking.

As the months passed, I stopped working in children's ministry and I began teaching two life groups on Sunday mornings for women. Instead of simply attending, I was now the co-teacher of the weekly Wednesday morning Bible study with Cindy. Even though I was happy with my new weekly activities, I couldn't keep from asking my what-if questions. They were questions that haunted me and were very dark: What if Bill had not had a breakdown? What if we had not had to retire? What if we can't find a medication to help him? What if he kills himself? What if I can't take this anymore? What if my life had not taken this path? What if I just quit? What happened to my life?

I found that stopping my what-if questions about Imani had been much easier than stopping the darker what-if questions I continued to ask myself about my life. I have served in women's ministry for over fifteen years. I have cried and prayed with women over their own painful what-if questions: "What if I had not miscarried my baby?" "What if my husband had not had that affair?" "What if I had not been abused as a teenager?" I found myself thinking about how I had handled those questions with hugs, prayers, tears, and listening. I was now in a position of needing hugs, prayers, tears, and listening myself, so God sent Kelly. A huge healing life lesson was about to happen when my friend Kelly took this what-if lesson to an even deeper level.

Kelly sent me a text message one afternoon telling me she had finished her training to become a life coach. A life coach is trained to help people improve relationships, clarify goals, and identify obstacles holding them back, and then work with them to create strategies to overcome their obstacles. A life coach is not a counselor or therapist who offers help with mental health and emotional healing but rather asks questions about goals and helps people focus on those goals. Kelly had finished her training and needed some people to sign up for coaching as a part of her internship. When she texted me and offered to coach me for three months at a greatly reduced fee, I agreed. I thought I was doing Kelly a favor, but I soon discovered that God had a plan to use her to challenge me. It was time for me to stop living in the what-ifs and learn a new lesson.

Kelly could see that I was stuck from the first moment we sat down to talk. I described my life as comfortable and manageable. She began to ask me about goals and dreams, and my answer was always, "I am trying to stay focused on this moment and trying to keep my head above water. I can't think about goals or the future." She suggested, "Let's start with something tangible, like goals of eating healthier and getting more exercise." I agreed.

As our sessions continued, life remained hard. Each time we met it seemed like I was in tears asking my dark what-if questions. She helped me realize I was experiencing grief at the loss of my own identity; somehow I felt less-than because of Bill's mental illness. I realized that people looked at and treated me differently because of his struggles. My marriage had changed because of the illness; I now felt more like a caretaker than a wife, and I was now a retired pastor's wife.

During one of our sessions, she asked me a question that would begin the healing process and challenge me out of my comfort zone of keeping everything manageable. She asked me, "If you could change anything about your life today, what would it be?" I answered without hesitating. I knew exactly what I would change. I would remove the pressure and struggles from the past four years. Bill would never have suffered depression. Suicidal thoughts would not have been a part of our lives. We would not have retired. We would not have gotten so far into debt because of the medical bills not covered by insurance. I wouldn't live with my daughter. I wouldn't live with the fear that the suicidal thoughts would come back. I wouldn't worry about Bill not getting better. I wouldn't have lost my identity as a wife or a pastor's wife. I fired my answers off, one after another.

She listened, smiled, and then asked me a second question, "What do you love about your life right now?" As I began to think about the answer to the second question, I knew I was in trouble. My response to the second question was going to change my answers to the first question. I started to list all of things I loved about my life today—my church, my circle of friends, the two life groups I lead every week, my cat, teaching the Wednesday morning Bible study with my friend Cindy, my cute apartment, my garden full of flowers, my fruit trees, the hummingbirds in my yard, being so close to my children and grandchildren, and the freedom retirement had brought to have Disneyland passes and to travel. There was so much more I could have said, and all of these things were in my life *because* of the pressure and struggles of the past four years.

I saw it now. I couldn't remove those struggles without losing all the things I had come to love. My focus shifted from the pressure and pain of the journey to all the beautiful things I have in my life. My response helped me move from living in the what-ifs to recognizing what I have. What-if living is a mindset of dwelling on all the things I don't have. Living with a focus on what I have means I am right where God wants me.

James 4:13–14 speaks of situations where we tell God our plans—where we are going to go and what we are going to do when we get there. God replies by saying, *You don't know the first thing about tomorrow.* God shows us the best way. James writes, "Instead, make it a habit to say, 'If the Master wills it and we're still alive, we'll do this or that'" (James 4:15).

As I read the verses, I heard God make a statement and ask me a question. He told me that I must live in this moment, for it is all I am guaranteed. He then asked me, *Are you telling Me what you're going to do, or are you asking Me for direction?*

Up to this point of my journey, I had always shared openly about my life taking a detour. Just like the missing ear had changed the life path of my cat, my life had taken a different path because of Bill's struggles with anxiety, depression, and suicidal thoughts. Now I understood it wasn't a detour at all. God has a plan, and He is using me in the middle of my mess. I am finding joy, and I am serving Him in ways I never would have had the opportunity to otherwise. Imani is not missing out because of her ear; she is living a life full of love and comfort. When she stares at me with those beautiful, green eyes, I believe she is exactly where she wants to be. In the same way, I am not missing out on life because of the struggles Bill is facing; I am living a richer, fuller life because of them.

# 10

## Leaning into God and His Truths

*If you don't know what you're doing, pray to the Father.*
*He loves to help.*

James 1:5

**The most important lesson Imani has taught me is the one** that has had the greatest impact on how I live my life. As a kitten she was mischievous, always stealing things off my desk and chewing on wires. I started putting any small items from my desk into drawers to keep her from stealing them, and I filled a squirt bottle with water to use when I caught her chewing. At three years old, though she's no longer a kitten, she will still steal pens, paperclips, sticky note-pads, and my reading glasses that I forget to put in drawers, and I will find the items hidden under my bed. I was still using the spray bottle to reprimand her until I noticed it was no longer having the effect I desired.

Imani was sitting on the floor of my office, and she had pulled the cord for a floor lamp out from behind a bookcase. As she laid there, playing with and chewing on the cord, I picked up the squirt bottle and pointed it right at her. I was about to pull the trigger and squirt her when I saw the look on her face and burst into laughter. This crazy cat had it all figured out.

As the bottle was pointed right at her face, she braced her body and squinted her eyes. She knew the spray of water was coming and that it would be over soon. Why give up her play when she could simply brace herself, squint, and live through it, knowing that in a few moments it would be over? I watched her do the same behavior over the next week every time the spray bottle came out. She wanted to play, to chew, and the spray of water didn't bother her enough to stop. She could brace and squint right through the process. I realized that I had to change the method I was using to get her to stop chewing.

I figured out that she hates loud noises, so I now use a small fly swatter and hit the carpet when I need her to stop chewing. I never come near her with the fly swatter, but the movement and the noise of it hitting the carpet have caused her to stop. No bracing or squinting. I have even noticed that she won't return to the spot to chew, and most of her chewing has stopped altogether. I found a way to discipline her that worked.

As I sat thinking about my cat bracing and squinting, my picture changed as I remembered an experience from when my children were very young. This experience taught me about friendship, and it also taught me about how each one of us is different in how we respond to discipline, problems, and messes. Bill and I had always been united when it came to the discipline of our children. When Kate was five and Jack was three, we discovered in a quite painful yet comical way that they were going to require different standards of discipline.

In our early years of ministry, we would spend every Sunday evening with our friends, Delynn and Wolfgang. Bill had known Wolf since grade school, and I had been friends with Delynn since seventh grade. We each went to different churches, and after our Sunday evening services, we would drive to their home. Dinner was whatever leftovers were in their refrigerator, and then we would put all our kids to bed. My children slept upstairs in their master suite, and the adults would play games and visit until late into the evening.

One evening while we were playing games, we heard Kate and Jack giggling upstairs. Bill went up to check on them, and I can still remember his face as he walked to the catwalk overlooking the family room where the three of us were sitting. He looked down at Delynn and said, "Please tell me you are removing the wallpaper in your bedroom?" Delynn looked up and said, "No, my, mom just finished putting it up a few days ago." Bill went pale and said, "I think you need to come up here."

We could all tell that a major wallpaper disaster had taken place. My lesson on friendship came with her next statement. "Bill, nothing your children have done is going to ruin our friendship. Come back down and let's finish the game." I couldn't stand it anymore, so I bolted up the stairs to see the damage. The wallpaper went halfway up the wall and had a wooden border across the top seam. My children had pulled the wallpaper off a six-foot section above their bed, shredding it as they pulled. I was mortified.

I walked into the room as Kate and Jack began to cry, and I saw Bill was preparing to spank them. Our children have always been so different in personality, and that night our method of discipline for each of them changed. Kate, willing to take her punishment, stretched out on the bed face down, crying as Bill swatted her. The minute Bill delivered the last swat, she stopped crying. Jack was another issue. Bill kept trying to get him to roll over so he could swat him. When he finally rolled over, it was a wrestling match to get his hands out of the way.

I stood watching as Bill continued struggling to get Jack's hands out of the way so he could swat him. Kate took matters into her own hands. She got down on the floor and looked up at Jack's face hanging over the edge of the bed. She looked up at him and said, "Stop fighting and take your punishment like a man; it will all be over in a minute, and it will stop hurting really fast." Bill and I looked at each other trying not to laugh. Kate had figured out what I later saw Imani doing. Bracing and squinting, because it will be over quickly.

We tucked the kids back into bed and wandered downstairs. I got the information on the wallpaper so I could order some more, and we had a great laugh over Kate's comments. It meant so much to me that Delynn never left her chair that evening to assess the damage. It cemented in my heart that she was one of those I-am-always-here-no-matter-what friends. To this day, I know she prays for me and is there if I need her.

The next day I ordered the wallpaper, then Bill and I began to discuss the changes we needed to make in disciplining our children. We decided that the best way to discipline Kate was to remove her from the party and send her to her room. It didn't matter if the party was only a family dinner. She hated to miss anything. The threat of removal became punishment enough. No more swats for her. Jack responded to the threat of a swat. We rarely ever followed through because just the thought of a swat caused him to rethink his behavior.

Imani, Kate, and Jack are like you and me. Each one of us responds differently to discipline and pain. We all brace and squint in our own ways. Imani and Kate knew the pain would pass quickly, but Jack would brace and squint to avoid the pain. None of them were learning the lesson needed until we found a method that worked for each of them. The point of discipline is change, and since pain is different for each of us, it has to get bad enough to make those needed changes.

A few months later, the wallpaper had been replaced, and we were putting the kids to bed on a Sunday night. As we shut off the light and were walking out of the room, we heard Kate say to Jack, "I am not going to touch the wall." Jack replied, "Not me either." Lesson learned. Bill and I smiled at each other as we walked downstairs.

One afternoon the cycle of Bill's anxiety was causing him negative control issues once again. I could tell that the blaming-me part was coming next, and I felt the tension building up in my body. All of a sudden, the picture of my tiny cat, then my children, bracing and squinting, came into my mind. I found myself asking God, *Is this what I am doing? Am I bracing and squinting, because I know if I can just get through this, it will pass until the next time? Do I need to learn to do something different?* God's answer to me in that moment was, *Girl, stop bracing and squinting, and start leaning into Me. Use the coping skills you have learned. I am right here with you!*

James 1:5 says, "If you don't know what you're doing, pray to the Father. He loves to help." Instead of anticipating, bracing, squinting, or waiting for the anger and blame to start, I now look inside at the emotional storm raging in me and evaluate every thought. *I feel like a failure because I don't know what to do. I feel the shame and embarrassment of what people will think.* Or I begin to believe the lie that I am the one responsible for Bill's actions. As I face each thought, I stop bracing and squinting for the coming pain. Instead, I start praying to God, asking, *God, what I should do? Your Word in James tells me You love to help.* By doing this, I stop bracing and squinting, and I lean into God. I go back to the truths I have learned, the ones He has taught me over and over. He is right here with me. He knows exactly what is going on. I recall how He has shown up before through care from others, taking care of our financial needs, showing me how to cope in practical ways, and telling me what to do. As the truth becomes clearer, I calm down, and my attitude changes and so do my actions and reactions.

I brace and squint when I feel responsible for Bill's pain. When I feel anger and blame coming, realizing I can't fix or avoid it, I start telling myself that I don't deserve the treatment. I react to what I think is coming. But I lean into God when I tell myself, *Stop it. You are not responsible. You can't fix this. Trust God and love Bill.* I am learning to lean into God and live in the moment, knowing God will show me what to say and do.

When I feel alone and scared, when the fear creates a fog in my brain so thick I can't think or find my way out, I start bracing and squinting. But if I lean in and make a phone call to my therapist or one of my close friends and tell them how I feel, they point me right back to the truth: I am not alone, and God is closer to me than anyone else.

When the grief of all that has been lost overcomes me and I find myself, crying, yelling, or even screaming at God, I am bracing and squinting. I lean in when I remember that God will lovingly handle any emotion I throw at Him. After the moment of grief passes, I pull away into a quiet place where I sit and listen as God reminds me of every time He has been there. I lean in and reflect on all He has done.

The difference between bracing, squinting, and leaning in is a simple one. When I brace and squint, I am trying to do it on my own. My thoughts progress to something like, *I can do this. It will be over soon. You have been here before. You don't deserve this. This is unfair. I want my life back.* I usually make it worse by saying something out of my pain and anger. Bracing and squinting makes the circumstances worse.

When I am leaning in, my focus moves away from my mess and Bill's illness, and I begin asking for help. My thoughts and prayers are, *God tell me what to say. Tell me what to do. I know Bill is in pain. It's not me. How should I respond?* Leaning in usually diffuses the situation, and God sends help. Why? Because my God loves to help!

The question is, how do you learn your lessons? Do you brace and squint, hoping it will pass quickly so you can get on with life? Or do you lean into God and remember the truths and lessons He has taught you?

I know dealing with someone who struggles with mental illness can be difficult. The answers and ways to help are not always going to be the same. You can't create an auto response that works every time; believe me, I've tried. So practically, what can you do? For my situation, I have created three possibilities to choose from when I am responding to Bill's anger, blame, or control:

1. I evaluate the situation by assessing. Is Bill tired, hungry, angry, or stressed? How much sugar or caffeine has he had?

All of these affect his mood swings. Once I evaluate, I can respond to his need.

2. I let Bill talk. He can talk for as long as he needs and say whatever he needs to say. If he is angry and his blame is focused on me, then I use my palms-up or loving-three-seconds-at-a-time methods to help me get through it.

3. I know my limits. If I am running on empty, emotionally or physically, I have to find a way to distract Bill. Most of the time now, I can suggest we watch a TV show, run an errand, or go for a walk. On rare occasions, when I have to walk away and remove myself, I make sure to the best of my ability that he is safe and not suicidal, then I remove myself until my resources are restored.

Isaiah 30:19–21 (NIV) is a Scripture I turn to when I am questioning if God will really tell me what to do. In these verses, Isaiah speaks about God's mercy to Israel. He basically tells Israel, no more tears. God hears and will answer as soon as He hears their cry. Isaiah then makes a reference to their teacher no longer being hidden. He is talking to the people about the Messiah, Jesus, and their ability to see Him with their own eyes. Verse 21 (NIV) says, "Whether you turn to the right or the left, your ears will hear a voice behind you, saying, 'This is the way, walk in it.'" In Isaiah's time, the Messiah had not yet been sent to us. But today we have the risen Messiah, who sits with God. We also have the Holy Spirit, who lives inside each of us who believe in Jesus Christ. He is right here with us, inside of us, in the middle of our mess with us, and He tells us in every circumstance which way to walk. God really does tell me what to do. He absolutely speaks. No bracing or squinting needed, only leaning in and listening.

# 11

## When It's Time to Reset

*You'll get his help, and won't be condescended to when you ask for it.*
James 1:5

**One afternoon my cell phone locked up and was not** responding. I knew that if I pushed a series of buttons the phone would reset, so I started the process. As I watched the screen of my phone go through the reset cycle, it hit me that I, too, was in need of a reset. I was isolating again, feeling all of the negative emotions that go along with Bill's illness: fear, resentment, anger, and exhaustion. It was time to regroup.

Isolation is my go-to behavior when the stress of caring for Bill gets too much for me to handle. I find myself pulling away from everyone, I don't read my Bible, I don't listen to my worship music, I turn off my phone, I stop checking email, I can't sleep, I can't get off the couch, I definitely eat more, and I become easily irritated. If I haven't taken a shower in over forty-eight hours and I am still in the same pj's or yoga pants, that is a good indication that I am in isolation and in need of a reset. I know someone who read that last sentence gets this and is nodding their head in agreement right now. During these times my focus is on me—and not in a good way.

Sometimes I feel like I am having an out-of-body experience, like I'm watching myself isolate and I'm not able to stop. The danger with stress and isolation, and the behaviors that go along with them, is that eventually my own health will begin to suffer. I have a sticky note taped to the window in my office that says, "Reset! If you don't take care of you, you won't be able to take care of anyone else." I realized as my phone cycled back on, that I had stopped taking care of myself. I was isolating and definitely in need of a reset. I wish it was as easy as pushing buttons on my phone.

Jack and his family had come to visit for a few days, and later that morning, I found myself on the back patio with Kate and LeeAnn. We were drinking coffee and watching the five children, Kate's three (Ty, eleven; Kinslee, nine; Henry, four) and LeeAnn's two (CJ, three; Liam, one), jump on the trampoline. The Bakersfield weather was already hot and sticky, so Kate had set a sprinkler under the trampoline. The water was spraying up through the mesh and created a cool, fun playground for the kids.

As I watched the kids playing and splashing in the water, I decided I wanted in on the fun. I set my coffee cup on the ground and walked over to the trampoline. I climbed up and crawled right into the middle of the fun. I saw five faces, ten eyes shocked to see me sitting in the middle of trampoline as the water flooded around us. We all sat there staring at each other for a few seconds, and the kids didn't know what to do. I looked down and saw the water pooling at my crossed legs, so I took my hands and with a swipe, I sent a wave of water that hit each of the kids in the face at the same time. I giggled at the shocked look on each face. Even the one-year-old was unsure of what to do next. Ty saw me put my hands down to splash them again, and he yelled, "Get MauMau!" The next thing I knew, I was tackled. As the six of us were bouncing and rolling around in the puddles of water; the laughter, screaming, yelling, and tackling was infectious. At one point I was on the bottom of all five kids.

I was resetting in the best way. For a few moments I forgot about my questions that had no answers and the dark, unknown, scary future. I was living in that moment, enjoying the love and fun of the known. I was MauMau to these five children. They loved me, we were having a blast, and, for now, that was enough. Resetting is similar to flipping a breaker switch and turning the power back on. Resetting attitudes puts emotions back to the way they were. Getting out of isolation or resetting means I look inside and make a choice. I flip an internal switch that means choosing to get off the couch and go for a walk, eat a banana instead of a candy bar, let go of the stress so I can sleep, call a friend to meet me for coffee or lunch, or play on the trampoline with my grandchildren.

I know this is hard. I have felt guilty at times when I am finding joy and laughter while Bill continues to struggle. It is extremely hard to be happy when someone you love is miserable and fighting the battle of mental illness. I go back to my sticky note posted in the window, "Reset! If you don't take care of you, you won't be able to take care of anyone else." I take care of me and that equips me, giving me the strength and stamina I need to then take care of Bill.

People often comment about my visits to Disneyland. Why do I, and how can I, go to Disneyland so often? When my husband was in the psychiatric hospital, how could I have gone three times? Because Disneyland is a reset for me. I love everything about the parks—rides, energy, colors, parades, characters, food, music, and fireworks. Even now as I think about Disneyland, a big smile comes across my face.

I remember my birthday last year. When it's your birthday at Disneyland, it is important to wear the button they provide. It says, "Happy Birthday, _____!" and you fill in your name. As I sat on the bench watching the afternoon parade, every character who walked by, but couldn't talk, came over or waved or gave me a heart symbol with their hands. The characters who could talk, yelled, "Happy Birthday, Carole!" Every ride operator, store clerk, or restaurant employee saw my button and wished me a happy birthday. If I could, I would spend every birthday at Disneyland.

On another visit, I ran into the pirate Jack Sparrow in front of the Pirates of the Caribbean ride. He walked over, put his arm around me, and asked, "Be we celebratin' anythin' today?" I told him, "Yes, my wedding anniversary." He looked at Bill, and asked me, "Be this yer ol' mate? Do ye love 'im?" I answered, "Yes." While Bill kept filming the encounter, Jack Sparrow renewed our wedding vows on the streets of New Orleans Square. "Do ye loot this strumpet t' be yer bride? Then, I pronounce ye ol' mate 'n' beauty." I love to reset at Disneyland anytime I can get there.

My favorite Disney quote is written on a sticky note on the window in my office and is attributed to Rafiki of *The Lion King*. "The past can hurt, but the way I see it, you can either run from it or learn from it." At one point in the movie, Rafiki looks at Simba the lion and says, "You have to put your past behind you." When CJ was three, he loved *The Lion King*. One day he was watching the movie and tried to repeat that quote by saying, "You have to put your behind in your pants." Yes, I have that one written on a sticky note on my window as well.

When I turned sixty, I declared that the rest of my life would be the laughing years. I was going to find ways to laugh and to laugh out loud. Laughter is so good for you; it relieves tension, burns calories, improves your mood, helps you connect with people, and helps you deal with difficult circumstances. Laughter is infectious and feels so good. Laughter is a great way to reset.

That day on the trampoline, I caught the neighbor looking over the fence to see what all the laughter was about. When our eyes met, she gave me a thumbs up with a huge smile on her face. Laughter has become my favorite reset. I now seek out ways to have fun and laugh out loud. Laughing out loud is cathartic and helps cleanse and purge. Jumping with my grandchildren on the trampoline and visits to Disneyland, especially if the visit includes the grandchildren, are two of the ways I have found to laugh out loud.

During the reset on the trampoline that day, I also began to thank God for two things. I had finally found a therapist to help me process and grow through the chaos of my husband's illness. I was also thankful because I had found things to do. In answer to my prayers, God brought Greg and Lynn into my life. That day on the trampoline, I thanked God for both of them. They both provide another way I reset in my life.

Before Bill went into the hospital, I had made a commitment to speak at three women's events. I was so tempted to cancel all three of them, especially the first one. It was too soon, we had no answers, and Bill had just gotten out of the hospital six weeks before. I could find so many reasons why I should not speak at any of these events. My friend Nancy knows me so well that she called me right after Bill got out of the hospital and told me she was concerned that I would cancel these upcoming events. She challenged me to do them. She told me that God was going to use me, and she would be right there on the front row of all three events, cheering me on. Bill got out of the hospital at the end of November. The first event was in early January and the next two were in May, and Nancy was there each time.

The final event in May was the hardest one, but it was also the one that brought my friend and therapist Greg back into my life. I was speaking at a retreat for ministers' wives. I had been asked to share from a transparent and honest place about my husband's struggles. I was already deep in isolation and feeling lost in my identity, and I knew this was going to be hard. As I stood to speak, I looked out into the room and saw two women. I knew God had a plan because the two women who caught my eye were Brenda, who had already walked so much of my story with me, and Nancy. They were sitting in the front row smiling. They inspired me to share that day and to talk about how God kept showing up for me. They told me that they knew there would be women in that room who needed to hear my story.

I could relate to the women in the audience because I knew very well what it was like to be a minister's wife. I equate it to being President of the United States or First Lady where you are on display, and there are always people who have an opinion about you. As a minister's wife, there are always people in the church who have an opinion about how you dress and how you act, and you seem to automatically become their role model for marriage, raising children, and Christian living. You feel like you have to be everything for them. Pastors and their wives are put on pedestals they will eventually fall from. Suffering from mental illness is unacceptable for church leaders.

Unhealthy expectations are placed on pastors and their wives not only by church members but also by each other. Ministers and their wives tend to duplicate these expectations by also comparing each other and even acting like the church members, with opinions and criticism of brother and sister ministers. The expectations and criticism from both within the church as well as by others who are in ministry are painful and divisive.

As I finished sharing that day at the retreat, I asked the women to pray for me. I was still trying to find a therapist to help me process what I was going through. When I finished a woman approached me and said she knew of the perfect counselor in Fresno, who used to be a pastor but was now a therapist. She said the therapist had helped with her daughter, and she was optimistic he could help me as well. I slid my journal across the table and asked her to write his name and phone number down for me. I knew as she began writing the name that it would be Greg. I love God's sense of humor, and He was showing it off in great form at this moment.

Greg was the pastor and the friend who had encouraged and influenced me to start speaking and blogging, and he was the first person who challenged me to share from a transparent place. He had overseen this retreat for many years. His wife and I had spent many of those weekends sharing a cabin. Greg knew my husband and me very well. He was the perfect friend and therapist to walk through this season of my mess with me. I smiled as I looked at his name and number in my journal. I wanted to pick up my phone and call right then, but I had to wait as I had no cell service.

The next morning as I was driving home, I pulled over and sent Greg a text as soon as I got to a place where my cell service returned. I told him how I had gotten his number and that my life was falling apart. I shared that Bill was struggling and that he had been hospitalized because of depression, anxiety, and suicidal thoughts. I asked if he could help me. I pulled back on to the road and continued home, and a few hours later I received his reply. It said, "I woke up this morning and realized this was the weekend of that retreat. I thought of you and wondered where you were and how you were doing. Then I picked up my phone and saw your text. Call me." I replied, "I can't call, if I hear your voice I will fall apart." He replied, "Come to Fresno on Tuesday of next week." He gave me the address of where to go, the time to arrive, and most importantly, he gave me hope. He wrote, "I can help you!"

Greg continues to be a part of my journey. His friendship and gifting as a therapist help me process my circumstances and guide me in the messiness, and then he points me right back to God. He closes every one of our sessions with prayer and reminds me all the time how much God loves me. God had finally answered my first prayer—I needed a therapist who can help. God sent Greg.

In answer to my second prayer, something to do, God brought Lynn into my life the first summer after what we now refer to as my husband's *crash*. She is the women's ministry director at Valley Baptist Church. She called me one day and invited me to coffee. As we sat drinking coffee, she told me that she was new to her position. She is friends with Kate and knew I had been involved in women's ministry as a leader for years. She asked if I would mentor her, and I told her I would love to. She began asking me questions, and it felt so good to talk about my favorite thing—ministry to God's girls. We talked about the different programs of the church and how best to reach, encourage, and teach the women. I told her I was helping Kate with children's check-in on Sunday mornings and was attending the Wednesday morning Bible study Cindy taught. She then asked me about my thoughts on women's retreats. I pulled out a napkin and started writing some thoughts down for her. I explained to her how much I loved women's retreats and the special ways God shows up when we get away and focus on Him for a weekend.

She then told me, "I don't just want your input, I want you to help me coordinate a retreat for the women at Valley." She said she had a date three months away, but she didn't have a venue, speaker, or theme. I said, "We had better get busy; we have a lot of work to do, and I would love to coordinate the women's retreat with you."

God used Lynn to answer my second prayer of giving me something to do. I was convinced when Bill crashed and we retired that my ministry days were over. I thought God was done using me, because we were no longer in ministry and I was an ordinary, broken person sitting in the pew each week. What I didn't know was that I was exactly where God needed me to be for the next season of my life and the next season of ministry. God used Lynn to show me that He was not done with me yet, and she introduced me to my beautiful *valley girls*. These women continue to open their hearts and lives to me. They love me, listen to me, encourage me, and help me heal. Every week now on Sunday mornings, I teach a life group Bible study for some of my valley girls called Joy Filled Women.

Finding Greg, Lynn, and my valley girls, and now leading Joy Filled Women, has brought people into my life who inspire me, love me, and encourage me. This has been an important step in my reset.

My phone continues to need a reset from time to time, and so do I. The best model for resetting, I learned from Jesus. He is the perfect example of how important it is to reset. Have you ever noticed in the Scriptures how many times we find that Jesus went away to pray and be alone with God? After Jesus feeds five thousand men with five loaves and two fish, we read in Matthew 14:23, "With the crowd dispersed, he climbed the mountain so he could be by himself and pray." Jesus heals a man with a crippled hand and then Luke 6:12 says, "At about that same time he climbed a mountain to pray. He was there all night in prayer before God." In Mark 1 we read that Jesus heals Simon's mother-in-law and then in verse 1:35,

"While it was still night, way before dawn, he got up and went out to a secluded spot and prayed." Luke 5 tells the story of Jesus healing a man of leprosy and then in 5:16 we read, "As often as possible Jesus withdrew to out-of-the-way places for prayer." Following each miracle and healing, we see Jesus resetting by going alone to be with God and pray.

It is key that Jesus took time to pray and to be alone with God. His final act before He was arrested was to find a place to pray. Luke 22:39 (NIV) says, "Jesus went out as usual to the Mount of Olives, and his disciples followed him." Then he prayed alone when he reached the garden. "He withdrew about a stone's throw beyond them, knelt down and prayed" (Luke 22:41 NIV). Jesus was facing a painful few days that would end with His death on the cross, and what did He do? He found a place to be alone and talk to God.

I have begun to follow this same practice, and I call it *solitude time with God*. My favorite solitude spot is the beach. I set aside four hours, I bring my chair, Bible, journal, pen, and water, and I turn off my phone. The minute I step onto the sand, I don't speak for the entire four hours, and I sit quietly staring at the waves and listen. I open my Bible and read passages I have picked out already. Sometimes I write questions on the pages of my journal as they float into my mind. I write things in my journal that God says to me. Most of the time I sit quietly, basking in the glory of His creation and presence, listening and resetting.

The reset process for me starts with acknowledging I need it. Then I might ask for help and call Greg. I almost always figure out ways to laugh out loud, reach out to people who encourage and inspire me, or spend extended solitude time with God. Serving in the ministries I am involved with is also important in resetting. Most of the time, I end up choosing a combination of these. They all help me flip that internal switch to get back to living in the present. Reset helps me keep going, regroup, refocus, and find those moments of strength and calm in the messiness of my life. I encourage you to find things like I have to help you reset too.

# 12

## Knee Deep in Joy

*Joy does not simply happen to us.*
*We have to choose joy and keep choosing it every day.*

—Henri J. M. Nouwen

It took me over two years, but I finally said the words, "My husband suffers from mental illness." These were the hardest words I had ever spoken. Why? Because while we can talk about cancer, heart disease, the flu, or any number of ailments, there is an unresolved gag order when it comes to mental illnesses. When people do speak of mental illness, many do so from an ignorant place, without the tools to understand it.

I was one of those ignorant people, until mental illness became a part of my everyday life and attacked someone I love. As Bill began to struggle, it changed the way I viewed anxiety, depression, and suicidal thoughts because they affected him and the way we lived our lives. Over time my view of bipolar disorder, schizophrenia, and personality disorders changed as well. Mental illness is an umbrella for many conditions, all of which attack the mind. This is a dangerous group of illnesses because they change the way a person thinks about themselves and their identity, and it changes the way a person interacts with the people they love. The disease alters their perception of reality, challenges their ability to process thoughts and experiences, and leaves a trail of chaos, hurt, confusion, and anger in its wake.

So what changed? I did. As I researched mental illness, talked to doctors, and lived with Bill and watched him struggle, I began to understand what I was dealing with: an illness. With my understanding came my acceptance—mental illness is just that, an illness; it's time for all of us to treat it that way.

Even though I have no answers, I understand that while mental illness changes Bill's behavior and the way he deals with life, the man I have loved for so many years is still inside, even when I don't recognize him. Bill is not doing and saying the hurtful things on purpose; he really can't help himself.

The next thing that changed? In a moment of clarity, Bill accepted his illness. Bill had finished reading a part of my manuscript for this book one day, and I could tell something was bothering him. I asked him if he was okay, and he said, "It bothers me that everyone is telling me I am mentally ill." I asked him, "If you had cancer and were going through chemotherapy, would you feel the same way? If you had diabetes and needed insulin, would you feel the same way? Is there any illness you could imagine having where you would feel what you are feeling right now?" He thought about it for a minute and said, "No, it's just mental illness. Somehow this makes people look at me differently." I asked him a question, "Where does mental illness originate?" He said, "My mind. I have an illness in my brain." He then quietly said, "Write this book, tell them! Start a conversation that will force change. Help the people who love those of us who have mental illness."

When Bill first came out of the hospital, in my initial pain I told my story to anyone who would listen. In those early days, while I was searching for answers, encouragement, and support, I was transparent about my fears, pain, and questions, and I made people uncomfortable with my quest. I knew that it was time for the world, especially the Christian world, to start talking. I found out very quickly, I was not the only one who was living with someone who suffered from mental illness. I was, however, one of the few who would talk about it. One day I was telling my story to a woman, and she asked me, "Just how common is mental illness? Is it really such a big deal?" I had nothing to say to her that day. This question drove me to research. I began to look for an answer to her question, and I found out mental illness is, indeed, a really big deal!

Here are some mental illness statistics from 2018: "One out of every five people, will experience a mental illness struggle in any given year, and one out of two people will suffer from a mental illness in their lifetime."[8] These two statistics alone show that every person alive either knows someone who suffers from mental illness or is struggling with it themselves. Yet we continue to be silent, afraid to talk, embarrassed to admit to it, and most of the cases are left undiagnosed and untreated. The effects of our silence are seen in the suicide rates. In 2018 suicide was the second leading cause of death in people ages 10–34 and the fourth leading cause of death in people 35–54.[9] Here is another statistic that took my breath away. In 2018, there were two-and-a-half times more suicides (48,344) in the United States than there were homicides (18,830).[10] This is staggering to me—more than twice as many people killed themselves than those who killed another person. One more statistic I found from a report published in October 2017 suggested if the effects of mental illness could be prevented, there would be 6.7 million fewer divorces and 3.5 million more marriages over an eleven-year period of time.[11]

Christians and ministers are not exempt from these numbers. We all need to be concerned, really concerned, about these statistics. We need to stop looking at the numbers as bars or lines on a chart or graph and recognize that each number represents a human being, a relationship, a family. It is time to attach a human face to each number, someone God loves. I am confident that when the same statistics for 2020 are revealed, these numbers will unfortunately be higher because of COVID-19.

So how do we change this stigma and start talking? We first have to pull back the veil of secrecy and shame attached to mental illness. How can we begin the dialogue and start the process of finding answers if we're not willing to talk about it? We must consider mental illness as just that—an illness that can be diagnosed and treated. We must also accept that mental illness, unlike other illnesses, is not as easily diagnosed and treated. I asked a neurologist at one of my husband's appointments if he could tell which part of Bill's brain was causing his mental illness? The neurologist rolled his eyes sarcastically and answered, "Not without an autopsy."

I was offended, but as I walked out of the office, the thought crossed my mind: mental illness deals with a part of the body that we cannot do a biopsy on. This makes it harder to diagnose and treat, because we can't examine the organ and see the illness until the person has died. When people die of cancer, diabetes, and COVID-19, we say the disease took their life, or the person got tired of fighting the illness. When you suffer from mental illness, death is usually caused by suicide. It feels so much more personal. We think that the person should have been able to control the illness, to fight. At the funeral of someone who committed suicide, I heard one of the guests comment, "_____ should have made a better choice." This made me so angry. It felt like they were saying a person chooses to suffer from mental illness. I promise you that is not the case. I know that in my husband's situation, he would give anything to not have to deal with the anxiety, depression, and suicidal thoughts. And without medication he has not been successful in controlling his thoughts. We can't explain mental illness away, and we can't will it away.

Like other illnesses, we must continue searching for help, treatments, and healing. Nowhere will you read or hear me say this is easy. It's not! This illness is a very formidable foe. The only way I can deal with it is knowing that I have God on my side, helping me, walking through it with me, and sending other believers to help me. I had to work through my anger, fear, and disappointment, and I had to accept it was an illness myself, before I could start the journey of helping others.

Now that I feel comfortable in the dialogue about mental illness, I can encourage others to open up and talk. In case you're wondering, I do not just walk up and say, "Hi, I'm Carole, and my husband struggles with mental illness." I am much more subtle. When asked where I am from, I will usually answer, "When my husband was forced to retire, we moved to Bakersfield." Almost always this leads to, "Why was he forced to retire?" The door is left wide open, so I say, "My husband struggles with mental illness, anxiety, depression, and suicidal thoughts."

January 1, 2020, was the start of a new year and a new decade! It was also a continuation of year five of our messy journey with my husband's struggles with still no answers and no resolution. Thankfully we do have a medication that keeps the suicidal thoughts away most days.

In February, I met a woman who is national speaker, author, and seminary professor. We were both teaching at a conference, and when we were introduced, she asked me, "Where do you live?" It worked perfectly, I said, "We moved to Bakersfield when my husband was forced to retire." I could tell she was going to go there, and she did. She said, "Forced to retire?" I said with a big smile, "Yes, my husband struggles with mental illness; his anxiety, depression, and suicidal thoughts forced him to retire." I loved what she said next, "I am finding myself really sorry I asked you that question right now, but go on." We were interrupted a few minutes later, and she was ushered away. I think she might have signaled someone to save her from me. I hope that she remembers our encounter, especially my smile and transparency. The statistics show she knows or is someone who struggles with mental illness. I pray if I ever run into her again, she will be open to conversation.

A few days ago, a photo popped up as a memory on one of my social media pages. It brought a smile to my face as I sat for a few moments remembering the day and circumstances where the photo was taken. The photo was of my son and me. We were standing in the middle of a grassy field, and he was standing behind me. He had his hands on my hips guiding me, and we were both looking up staring at the beautiful, blue sky. Our family has always been very competitive and athletic. I am definitely competitive, but all athletic ability skipped me. I figured out very early in my life that sports of any kind were not in my wheelhouse, so I was always the designated cheerleader, sitting on the sidelines and cheering everyone else on.

On the day this photo was taken, our family was in the park playing Wiffle ball, and I was sitting on the sidelines as usual. Jack kept trying to get me to join in the fun and get in the game. He encouraged me, saying he would teach me to catch, and he knew I could do it. Finally I decided I would do it. I got out of my chair and walked into the outfield. I remember he grabbed my waist and told me, "Put your hands up, Mom; keep your eye on the ball," and then he gently moved me into position. Bill then hit a ball that was coming straight toward me, and I caught it! The celebration dance was epic. I was so excited! I gave Jack a big hug, as he said, "I knew you could do it, Mom!"

As I sat staring at that photo, I remembered that feeling of joy and the sense of accomplishment. I chose to get up out of my chair that day and put myself into the game. I allowed Jack to coach me and guide me to the exact spot I needed to be in. Success came because I was willing to accept help and try.

The year 2020 has brought a new challenge to deal with. In March, Bill and I were at Disneyland when the park announced it would be closing in two days because of COVID-19. Disney planned to keep the park closed for one month, but as I write this, the park has been closed now for ten months, with no opening date in sight. COVID-19 has brought fear and change. People are terrified of getting sick and possibly dying. Isolation and social distancing have become words we use every day. My grandchildren go to school online, our church meets outside on the grass, lunch dates with my husband are curbside pickup and eating in our car. There are so many more changes that COVID-19 has brought. The virus has also brought a dangerous rise in mental illness, stress, fear, anxiety, and depression. They are all at an all-time high.

A survey entitled *America's State of Mind Report* highlighted that from February 16 to March 15, when COVID-19 was just beginning, filled, weekly prescriptions for antidepressants, antianxiety, and anti-insomnia medications had increased by 21 percent.[12] Here is the most interesting part of this report: 78 percent of all three of the above prescriptions filled during the week of March 15, when our country began to shut down, were new prescriptions, not refills. I will share only one suicide statistic: Fresno, California, reported that in June 2020, the number of suicides was 70 percent higher than June 2019.[13] I have personally talked with and prayed for five people who have been touched by suicide in their families.

Now as I begin a new day, a new year, and a new decade, I decided there is no more sitting on the sidelines—no more waiting or trying to ignore or change my circumstances. When I chose to stand up and get into the game that day with Jack coaching me, it was so much more than just playing Wiffle ball. I was choosing joy, and I was asking for help. I was letting some incredible people step up to guide and teach me. As I look at the photo again of Jack teaching me to catch, I imagine the faces of all the incredible people that God has put in my life to encourage and support me and my husband on this journey of mental illness. I am so thankful for each one.

These past five years have been chaotic, scary, and overwhelming. We still have no clue as to why my Bill began to suffer from depression and suicidal thoughts in 2016. We have begun to explore some family genetics and his anxiety as a child, and our journey for answers continues. Today the depression is controlled by medication, and he tries to manage his anxiety by reading, therapy, and trying to calm himself down with self-talk. The suicidal thoughts are rare because the medication helps control the anxiety and depression.

I have come to the realization that this journey may continue for the rest of Bill's life. Two years ago when things were at their darkest, someone I trust asked me this question, "Why do you stay?" It took me months to finally understand why they asked me the question and what my answer would be. They asked me the question because when things are at their darkest, I have to be able to go back and look at the reasons I stay. I have the reasons written on a sticky note on my window, a place where I can access them quickly. I have looked at the reasons many times, crying, screaming, and begging God for a different answer. My reasons are:

> I will stay because I made a vow before God to love and honor my husband in sickness and in health, for richer or poorer, until death do us part. Nothing in these vows has changed!

> My joy, my love, my commitment is to God first, my husband second. The first commitment to God gives me the strength to do the second.

> I stay because I love my husband.

> I stay because I want my children and grandchildren to know what true commitment to God, spouse, and family looks like.

So today might be a day that I am trudging along, or it might be a day I am skipping. It is definitely a day that I am knee-deep in a mess, and the joy is flowing.

*I love, I hurt, I love again . . .*
*I hurt, I heal, I hurt again . . .*
*I heal, I question, I heal again . . .*
*I question, I trust, I question again . . .*
*I trust, I lean in, I trust again . . .*
*I lean in, I stay, I lean in again . . .*
*I stay, I stay for good!*

# Carole's Survival Tips and Tools

**A survivor is a person who finds ways to cope when life** becomes messy. You may have read through this book highlighting tips and tools and things you want to remember. But when chaos and messiness hit, when you have those times where you really need the tips, it's difficult to remember or find the information.

I wanted a place where the information could be easily accessed when crisis hits and when you are in survival mode. Here you can find an overview of each chapter, along with these elements:

> Truths—Lessons and truths from each chapter
>
> Scripture—Bible references I use
>
> Sticky-Note Moments—Things I have written on notes and stuck on my office window
>
> To-Do List—Actions and questions that might help you process your mess and find joy

I have also included a list of songs and artists from my "When Life Gets Scary" playlist, some resources I use daily in my life, and a special shout-out to some people who help me in specific ways. I hope you will find this information helpful on your own journey to find joy in your mess.

**Introduction**

Truths
- I was desperately in need of rescuing and God showed up.
- A personal relationship with Jesus was my first step.
- God loves us all just the way we are.
- God has a plan for our lives that only we can fulfill.
- We all drag trunks full of emotions and painful experiences into our adult lives and relationships.

Scripture
- I don't reference this Scripture in the introduction, but John 3:16 is the passage the pastor was preaching from the night I met Jesus. Read this passage in *The Message* and insert your name.

Sticky-Note Moments
- "Life can only be understood backwards; but it must be lived forwards." — Søren Aabye Kierkegaard
- You are not alone; God sees you and I see you.
- The journey will be daunting and overwhelming. Take a deep breath, focus for a moment on something that makes you smile, and keep going. You can do this; we can do this together.
- God loves me just the way I am.
- There is nothing I have ever done or will do to make God stop loving me.

To-Do List
- Do you believe that God loves you just the way you are?
- Identify what is in the trunks you have been dragging through life.
- Start unpacking those trunks. Begin to read your Bible daily.
- Ask God how He plans to use the mess in your life.
- Will you embrace God's plan for your life?

**Chapter 1: How Could This Happen to Bill?**

Truths

- Mental illness is a cycle. There are up and downs.
- We as Christians need to begin talking openly about mental illness.
- We need to focus on the gift of God's presence instead of on the mess.
- Learn from Paul. Though he begged God to remove his issue, God wanted him to trust Him and to focus on His presence.

Scripture

- James 1:2–5
- 2 Corinthians 12:7–10

Sticky-Note Moments

- God says, "My grace is enough; it's all you need. My strength comes into its own in your weakness."
- God said, "You and Paul have so much in common, read his story."

To-Do List

- If your mess is due to mental illness in the life of a loved one, talk about it.
- Are you like Paul, focusing on a mess in your life instead of on the presence of God?
- Are you begging for answers, while God is telling you to trust Him?
- Will you choose joy in your mess, even without answers?
- Identify some ways God has walked before your mess, preparing the way.

**Chapter 2: Why Is This Happening?**

Truths

- God says, "When challenges come, I am right there with you. I have a plan."

- Sometimes a concentrated look at a portion of the Scripture is all you can handle.
- Your mess will force your faith-life out into the open.
- God will show you what to do and fill you with joy.

Scripture

- James 1:2–5
- 1 Kings 19:1–4
- Psalm 16:11 (NIV)

Sticky-Note Moments

- God says, "Here I am, I see you. I will be with you. I will carry you."
- Joy = A state of happiness or bliss
- "Joy is the settled assurance that God is in control of the details of my life." —Kay Warren
- "You make known to me the path of life; you will fill me with joy in your presence." (Psalm 16:11)

To-Do List

- Keep reading the Bible. Focus on a small portion of Scripture if that's all you can handle.
- What portion of Scripture will you focus on?
- Consider your mess a gift, and keep trusting.
- Identify your mess. Will you begin to consider it a gift and a part of God's plan for your life?
- How do you see your faith being put on display because of your mess?

## Chapter 3: Facing Emotional Tumbleweeds

Truths

- God says, "Challenges will come!"
- When the challenges come, He is right there with us.
- We must ask the right questions.
- You are not alone. God sees you.
- When God sends people, let them in.

- God uses people like you and me to help people like you and me.

Scripture

- James 1:2
- Psalm 5:11

Sticky-Note Moments

- God says, "Take a deep breath. I am here, rest in me."
- God says, "You are right where I want you to be, I am proud of how you're handling this, and I have a plan."
- "Okay, this is happening, now what?"
- "You'll welcome us with open arms, when we run to you for cover." (Psalm 5:11)

To-Do List

- Are you asking the wrong question: *Why is this happening?*
- Begin thinking, *Okay, this is happening, now what?*
- Search for that joy tumbleweed in the pile of scary ones.
- Do you feel alone? Identify the people God has sent and let them in.
- Take a deep breath and run to God for cover.

## Chapter 4: The Source of My Strength, Power, and Joy

Truths

- Trust in God, not your stuff.
- God is our source of strength, power, and joy.
- He will take care of us.
- Ask boldly, "Show me, God, what to do." Expect Him to show up.
- Like Peter, we need to keep our eyes on Jesus, not on our mess.
- While we demand answers and tell God what we need, He demands our total surrender to Him and wants us to trust Him completely.

Scripture

- Nehemiah 1–6

- Nehemiah 8:10
- James 1:5
- Psalm 119:97–120
- Psalm 119:105 (NIV)
- Matthew 14:22–34

Sticky-Note Moments

- "The joy of the Lord is your strength." (Nehemiah 8:10)
- Clarity, Hope, Joy, Strength, Power. I have these written on individual notes.
- When I take my eyes off Jesus and focus on the mess, I begin to sink.
- God demands my total surrender to Him.
- I belong to the God of the Bible, and that is clarity enough for me.

To-Do List

- Boldly ask God to show you what to do.
- How is God helping you find normal and security in your mess?
- Where are your eyes fixed—on the mess or on Jesus?
- Are you demanding that God gives you answers?
- Will you respond to His demand for complete surrender to Him?
- Do you belong to the God of the Bible?

## Chapter 5: The Difference between Living in Fear and Living with It

Truths

- We must realize what is our responsibility and what is not.
- When we live *in* fear, we try to control circumstances out of our control.
- Change *What if?* to *"What now?*
- When we live *with* fear, we trust God.
- Using fear as a protector can inspire hands-on exercises such as:

- Creating a safe zone.
- Listening to worship songs and specialized playlists.
- Living with palms facing up.
- Using fear as a motivator can inspire:
  - Living in care, not control.
  - Loving three seconds at a time.

Scripture
- James 1:3
- Psalm 57:1–11

Sticky-Note Moments
- Let him go! Your job is to love him and trust Me!
- I can live *with* fear and not *in* fear, because I live with God.
- I must live in my safe zone.
- I live with my palms facing up.
- I will live in care, not control.
- I will love Bill three seconds at a time.
- Be good to me, God. I have run to you for dear life.

To-Do List
- Are you asking what-if questions? Begin to live in the moment and instead ask, *What now, God?*
- Is there a pressure you're feeling that you can't fix and is not your responsibility?
- Are you willing to place your mess in your palms, lift it up, and give it to God?
- Create a safe zone.
- Live with your palms facing up.
- What songs will you put on your "When Life Gets Scary" playlist?
- How can you live in care, not control?
- Who do you need to love three seconds at a time?
- Spend some quiet time reflecting on Psalm 57:1–11.

## Chapter 6: Facing the Opposition That Comes with Obedience

Truths

- People don't know what to say to you, so they walk away.
- Christian resources for mental illness are nonexistent.
- People can be judgmental when it comes to dealing with mental illness.
- Ask for help in discerning the truth when people say dumb things.
- Obedience to God is more important than people's comfort.
- God uses our stories; yours will help so many people.
- Isolation is not the answer.
- We can learn from the dumb things people say.
- Our faith-life is on display, and people can see God at work in our lives in a personal way.

Scripture

- James 1:3

Sticky-Note Moments

- It's not contagious!
- Is everyone staring at me? Yes, and I am going to point them to God.
- God said, "You heard me correctly. I am proud of how brave you have been."
- Keep trusting. Keep sharing. Keep choosing joy.
- I want my life to be a story that pulls you into it, cheering me on, while at the same time you wonder, "How is she not flat on the floor in a puddle?"

To-Do List

- Do you buy into the lie that if our lives are perfect, we are blessed, but if we have trials, there must be a hidden sin, and God must be angry with us?
- What dumb things have people said to you that you can use to evaluate your mess and learn from?

- Do you struggle with isolation? Who are you shutting out? Who do you need to let in?
- Are people staring? Is your faith-life on display?

## Chapter 7: God's Gift to Us Is in the Trials

Truths

- Trials and challenges have never shown up on anyone's gift wish list.
- God sees trials and challenges as a gift to help us grow.
- When we are afraid, we need to turn to God. Worship music is a great tool.
- God can remove our fears, even if the challenge remains.
- We can feel God's presence in creation.
- God speaks through storms, fire, a quiet whisper, and also through Google.
- Don't turn back out of fear; you will miss an adventure.

Scripture

- James 1:2
- Job 38:1
- Deuteronomy 4:12
- 1 Kings 19:13

Sticky-Note Moments

- I have learned from my messy life that God sees trials differently than we do. He sees them as a gift to help us grow.
- God says, "I am right here, and no matter what happens, you will be okay."
- God says, "I will be here to walk with you, holding you close; I will carry you when it gets hard. You must fight through your fears and trust Me."
- I have turned my fear of the trial into the anticipation of the journey.

To-Do List

- Since God considers tests and challenges a gift that help us grow, how are you growing through your mess?
- What trials and challenges are you facing that God is telling you to fight through and trust Him?
- What perfect gifts has God given you?
- Identify a place where you feel especially close to God in His creation. (Maybe it's at the beach or in the mountains or on your back porch.)
- How can you choose to move your focus from the fear of the trial to the adventure of the journey?
- Create your own "When Life Gets Scary" music playlist.

## Chapter 8: Mastering Mental Gymnastics

Truths

- Caregiver burnout is an illness that can affect those who care for loved ones struggling with mental illness.
- When you care for someone who struggles with mental illness, there is a delicate balance between the pressure, which can help you mature or potentially destroy you.
- There is more help for those who struggle with mental illness than for those who care for them.
- Mental illness is a cycle. It is easy to believe our loved one is on the upswing and then get gobsmacked when it happens again.
- Guilt and shame are two symptoms of caregiver burnout.
- We must train to survive and master mental gymnastics.
- Self-care is critical to mastering mental gymnastics.
- Training and survival are a choice.

Scripture

- James 1:4
- John 3:16

Sticky-Note Moments

- Did I take my emotional temperature today?

- "This is how much God loved Carole, He gave his son, his one and only son for her. And this is why, so Carole need not be destroyed, by believing in Jesus, Carole can have a whole and lasting life." (John 3:16)
- I am replacing guilt and shame with restoration.
- The thing that needs to change is me: get off the hamster wheel and get to work.
- Training is the activity of learning a new skill or behavior.
- Surviving is continuing to live in spite of difficult circumstances.
- Mastering is to gain control of or overcome.
- Disneyland as often as possible!

To-Do List
- Take your emotional temperature.
- Are you stuck running on a hamster wheel?
- Have you been gobsmacked?
- Think about what drives you to jump on that wheel again.
- Are you carrying around guilt and shame that don't belong to you?
- Write John 3:16 in your journal, inserting your name.
- What new skill or behavior do you need to learn to survive and master mental gymnastics in your messy life?
- How are you using self-care to train for mental gymnastics?
- Did you create your "When Life Gets Scary" playlist yet?

**Chapter 9: Learning to Live with What I Have**

Truths
- We must stop asking what-if questions.
- Our lives must go on in the mess: set goals, make plans, live.
- Set tangible goals.
- We experience grief when we care for someone with mental illness.
- There are wonderful things in our lives because of our mess.

- Our focus must shift from the pressure and pain of the mess to the beautiful things we have gained because of it.
- We love to tell God where we are going and what we are going to do. We must stop telling and start asking for direction.

Scripture
- James 1:4
- James 4:13–14

Sticky-Note Moments
- There are things in my life I love because of the pressures and struggles of the mess.
- Living with a perspective of gratitude for what I have means I am right where God wants me.
- Am I telling God what I'm going to do, or am I asking Him for direction?
- My life has not taken a detour.
- I am not missing out on life because of the struggles my loved one is facing; I am living a richer life because of it.

To-Do List
- What are your what-if questions?
- Set some tangible goals you can accomplish now.
- Are you grieving the loss of something?
- What have you gained from your mess?
- Where is your focus: on the mess or on the things you have gained?
- Ask God for direction.

## Chapter 10: Leaning into God and His Truths

Truths
- We brace and squint, knowing the pain will pass when we should be leaning into God.
- We all respond differently to discipline and pain.
- Leaning in means recalling how God has shown up before and then trusting Him in that moment.

- When we are bracing and squinting, we are trying to do it on our own.
- When we lean in, we ask God for help.
- As believers, we have the risen Messiah who sits with God, and we have the Holy Spirit living inside us.

Scripture
- James 1:5
- Isaiah 30:19–21 (NIV)

Sticky-Note Moments
- My God loves to help.
- Stop it! You're not responsible; you can't fix this.
- God will show me what to say and do.
- "Whether you turn to the left or the right, your ears will hear a voice behind you saying, 'This is the way, walk in it.'" (Isaiah 30:21 NIV)

To-Do List
- How do you respond to discipline and pain?
- How has God shown up in the past?
- Practice dealing with your loved one who struggles with mental illness with these options:
  - Evaluate the situation.
  - Let them talk.
  - Know your limits.
- Are you trying to do it on your own?
- Do you need to learn something different?
- How do you hear God speak?

## Chapter 11: When It's Time to Reset

Truths
- Reset. If you don't take care of you, you can't take care of anybody else.
- Finding ways to laugh and have fun is a great way to reset.
- Resetting is like flipping the breaker switch and turning the power back on.

- We must choose to reset and get out of isolation.
- We may find ourselves feeling guilty if we are finding joy and laughing while our loved one struggles, but joy and laughter are vital.
- Finding people who inspire you to live is an important reset.
- Reset by serving and using your God-given gifts and talents.
- Jesus reset by pulling away to a solitary place to pray and be alone with God.
- We must find a place to be alone and talk to God for extended solitude.

Scripture
- James 1:5
- Matthew 14:23
- Luke 6:12
- Mark 1:35
- Luke 5:16
- Luke 22:39, 41

Sticky-Note Moments
- Reset! If you don't take care of you, you won't be able to take care of anyone else.
- Spend every birthday, anniversary, any day at Disneyland.
- "The past can hurt, but the way I see it, you can either run from it or learn from it." —Rafiki, *The Lion King*
- "You have to put your past behind you." —Rafiki, *The Lion King* "
- You have to put your behind in your pants." —CJ
- Reset starts the minute I acknowledge that I need it.
- Reset helps me keep going, regroup, refocus, and find those moments of strength and calm in the messiness of my life.

To-Do List
- How do you take care of you?
- Identify what things make you laugh.

- Do you struggle with isolation? How can you flip that breaker switch and get out?
- Is guilt keeping you from laughing and having fun?
- What do you do, or where do you go, to reset?
- Who inspires you to live?
- How do you serve? If your answer is, "I don't," then how will you start?
- Where can you go to find solitude time with God?

## Chapter 12: Knee-Deep in Joy

Truths

- We must talk about mental illness.
- Mental illness is an illness that needs to be diagnosed and treated.
- Mental illness is a big deal. Here are 2018 US statistics:[14]
  - One out of five people will experience a mental illness.
  - One out of two people will struggle or know someone who struggles with mental illness.
  - Mental illness is the second leading cause of death in people ages 10–34.
  - Mental illness is the fourth leading cause of death in people ages 35–54.
  - There were two-and-a-half times more suicides in 2018 (48,344) than homicides (18,830).
- We need to start attaching faces to each number and start talking.
- It's not easy; mental illness is a formidable foe. It can be hard to find treatments, medications, and therapy that will help. It can be harder to convince our loved ones to accept treatment, medication, and therapy.
- We must accept help from our cheerleaders and try.
- The year 2020 has brought a new challenge to deal with—COVID-19. Here are some statistics:[15]

- Between February 16 and March 15, prescriptions for antidepressants, antianxiety, and anti-insomnia medications increased by 21 percent.
- The week of March 15, 2020, 78 percent of those prescriptions filled were new ones, not refills.
- Fresno, California, reported in June 2020 that the number of suicides was 70 percent higher than June 2019.

• Our first commitment must be to God, so we can honor our commitment to our loved one who struggles.

Scripture

• James 1:2–5

Sticky-Note Moments

• Success came because I was willing to accept help and try.
• I stay because I made a vow before God to love and honor my husband in sickness and health, for richer or poorer, until death do us part. Nothing in these vows has changed.
• I stay because I want my children and grandchildren to know what true commitment to God, spouse, and family looks like.

To-Do List

• Write your mess down in your journal, and then say it out loud.
• Who do you talk to?
• How will you start the dialogue? Create your opening line.
• Who are your cheerleaders?
• If you're sitting on the sidelines, what is keeping you there?
• Why do you stay? It is important to answer that question.

**Music Playlist: "When Life Gets Scary"**

1. "Never Give Up" by for King & Country
2. "The God Who Stays" by Matthew West
3. "Holy Spirit" by Charlin Neal
4. "Your Name Is Power" by Rend Collective

5.  "The Father's House" by Cory Ashbury
6.  "Surrounded" by Michael W. Smith
7.  "Do It Again" by Elevation Worship
8.  "Amazing God" by Lincoln Brewster
9.  "Battle Belongs" by Phil Wickham
10. "Yes, I Will" by Vertical Worship
11. "Happy Dance" by MercyMe
12. "While I Wait" by Lincoln Brewster
13. "Fight On, Fighter" by for King & Country
14. "My Hope Is Built" by Shane & Shane
15. "We Win" by MercyMe
16. "Oh, My Soul" by Casting Crowns
17. "I Know You're Here" by Carrie King
18. "It Is Well" by Bethel Music
19. "joy." by for King & Country
20. "Dance" by B. J. Putnam
21. "Famous For" by Tauren Wells & Jenn Johnson
22. "Even If" by MercyMe
23. "Just Be Held" by Casting Crowns
24. "You're Gonna Be OK" by Bethel Music

## Resources

Books

- *A Guide to Rational Living*, Albert Ellis, PhD and Robert A. Harper, PhD, Wilshire Book Company
- *Hope and Help for Your Nerves*, Dr. Claire Weekes, A Signet Book
- *Making Your Mind Magnificent*, Steven Campbell, Aviva Publishing
- *Change Your Brain, Change Your Life*, Daniel G. Amen, Random House

Blogs
- drleaf.com/blogs/news
- healthyplace.com/blogs/mentalillnessinthefamily
- .mhanational.org/being-effective-caregiver
- carolesjourney.com/blog

Bibles
- *The Tony Evans Study Bible*, Holman Publishing
- *The NIV/The Message Parallel Bible*, Zondervan Publishing

Devotional Books
- *Streams in the Desert*, by L. B. Cowman, Zondervan Publishing
- *Grace for the Moment,* by Max Lucado, J. Countryman Publishing
- *My Utmost for His Highest*, by Oswald Chambers, Discovery House Publishing

Websites and Podcasts
- verywellmind.com
- brainwarriorswaypodcast.com
- amenclinics.com
- nami.org
- Fresh Hope for Mental Health podcast
- ncbi.nml.nih.gov
- ajmc.com
- carolesjourney.com

## Shout-Outs

We need people to help us get healthy when life gets messy. Here are some of the people who help me.

- **Greg—my friend and therapist.** If you are caring for or love someone who is struggling with mental illness, I urge you to find a trained therapist to help you process. Because Greg has known me for many years, and has closely walked with me these past three years, he knows the story so I don't have to start over every time. There have been times I am in survival mode, talking to him, and I am able to stop in the middle and say, "Okay, we have been here before, and this is what you're going to tell me." I can feel his smile through the phone. As a Christian friend and therapist, his guidance, support, and encouragement have been a lifeline for me. He always points me back to my spiritual lifeline in God and prays for me. Thank you, Greg!

- **Kelly Clanton—my life coach.** The first time I sat down with Kelly, I was exhausted and worn out. She was able to ask me questions, which helped me identify some emotions I was not dealing with and some things I wanted to change. We then worked through the process of setting goals and a plan of how I was going to move forward. I love that she lovingly holds me accountable. Her coaching gave me the courage to pursue writing this book. It had always been a goal I felt was unreachable, so she helped me identify why I was scared to try and to see that God had a plan, and the book was a part of it. Thank you, Kelly!

- **John Thompson—my fitness coach.** I am new to Thompson Fitness. I have been telling myself for too long that I need to get in shape. My daughter works out here, and I have watched John coach her. She has never been this healthy, so I finally decided it was time for me, too, to get healthy. After one class, I knew it was for me. John is a knowledgeable and gifted coach. There is something about getting a high five after doing a hard exercise that makes the pain worth it. I had lofty goals for my first class: do at least five reps of each exercise in the amount of time given, don't pass out, don't throw up, and don't quit. I laid on the floor after a really hard exercise, asking myself, *What the heck have I signed up for?* John came over and gave me a hand and lifted me up off the floor. He said seven words to me with a big smile that changed my attitude, "Come on, Carole, you can do this." He has no idea how that statement has challenged me to do more than just get in shape. Thank you, John!

# Notes

1. google.com/search?q=definition+of+hope&o-q=&aqs=chrome.3.35i39l8.1018747471j0j7&sourceid=-chrome&ie=UTF-8

2. google.com/search

3. kaywarren.com/article/choose-joy-because-happiness-isnt-enough/

4. google.com/search.

5. google.com/search.

6. google.com/search.

7. google.com/search.

8. cdc.gov/mentalhealth/learn/index.htm.

9. nimh.nih.gov/health/statistics/suicide.shtml.

10. nimh.nih.gov/health/statistics/suicide.shtml.

11. link.springer.com/article/10.1007/s00127-017-1373-1.

12. ajmc.com/view/how-has-covid19-affected-mental-health-severity-of-stress-among-employees.

13. adn.com/nation-world/2020/08/11/pandemics-effect-on-already-rising-suicide-rates-heightens-worry/.

14. cdc.gov/mentalhealth/learn/index.htm.

15. ajmc.com/view/how-has-covid19-affected-mental-health-severity-of-stress-among-employees.

# ORDER INFORMATION

To order additional copies of this book, please visit
www.redemption-press.com.
Also available on Amazon.com and BarnesandNoble.com
or by calling toll-free 1-844-2REDEEM.

CPSIA information can be obtained
at www.ICGtesting.com
Printed in the USA
BVHW071613060421
604327BV00004B/267